Eight Bright Candles
Courageous Women of Mexico

Doris E. Perlin

Republic of Texas Press

Library of Congress Cataloging-in-Publication Data

Perlin, D. E., 1936-.
    Eight bright candles : courageous women of Mexico / Doris E.
Perlin.
       p.   cm. — (Women of the West series)
    Includes bibliographical references and index.
    ISBN 1-55622-390-0 (paperback)
    1. Women—Mexico—Biography.   2. Mexico—Biography.
    I. Title.   II. Series: Women of the West series (Plano, Tex.)
    CT3295.P47   1995
    920.72'0972—dc20
    [B]   95-14089
                                         CIP

Republic of Texas Press is an imprint of Wordware Publishing, Inc.
No part of this book may be reproduced in any form or by any means
without permission in writing from Wordware Publishing, Inc.

Printed in the United States of America

ISBN 1-55622-390-0
10 9 8 7 6 5 4 3 2 1
9502

All inquiries for volume purchases of this book should be addressed to
Wordware Publishing, Inc., at 1506 Capital Avenue, Plano, Texas 75074.
Telephone inquiries may be made by calling:

(214) 423-0090

CONTENTS

For my mother
and in memory of
my father

ACKNOWLEDGEMENTS

I am deeply grateful to the Dallas Public Library where I was privileged to be granted use of the Frances Sanger Mossiker Writers Study Room. I especially acknowledge the immeasurable help and encouragement I received during the writing of this book from the staff of the Humanities Division and from my fellow writers in the Writers Room. The staffs of the History and Social Science Division, the Texas/Dallas History and Archives, and the Interlibrary Loan Division provided generous assistance with research and various library services for which I am most appreciative.

I also am greatly indebted to the Daughters of the Republic of Texas, Texas History Research Library at the Alamo, for access to their material and permission to use and quote from this material, to the Goliad Chamber of Commerce, to the Texas State Archives for permission to use material from their files, and to the Nettie Lee Benson Latin American Collection at the University of Texas at Austin for access to their picture files.

My special appreciation to María Isabel Ruiz Pérez for countless hours of translating. To my family and friends for their valuable comments and technical assistance, I say thank you again and again. Most importantly, my thanks to my husband and children for their support, encouragement, patience, and understanding during this project.

INTRODUCTION

Dynamic blends of Indian and Spanish heritage enriched the history of the country of Mexico; yet, for hundreds of years, Mexican women were shackled by the strong patriarchal traditions of this heritage. A father's authority was beyond question. The strict moral code established by the church and prevailing family attitudes shielded daughters from the sins of the world. Women were obedient and uncomplaining. They had no voice.[1]

Economic and social conditions governed a woman's lifestyle, including her educational opportunities, activities, and advantages or disadvantages. For some, this meant life as a slave or on the street. However, because tradition, at every social level, decreed that a woman stay close to the home serving her family, it did not suggest weakness on her part. Her strength held the family together when the man of the household left for battle or other pursuits. With or without him, she proudly carried out the customs of her culture and passed them along to her daughters.[2]

Marriages were usually arranged, often for social or economic reasons. Love was not a consideration.[3] If a woman chose not to marry or a marriage could not be arranged, the convent offered protection. Upon leaving her father's home, the husband or church became master. Most women, if not content with this way of life, accepted it as a way to retain their respectability.[4]

Typically, women took no part in political affairs or events outside the home, although a woman's social class or wealth increased her sphere of influence.[5] There were those who refused to comply with conditions ordered by their men or society as a whole. From time to time, brave women fought for political freedom and raised their voices to improve life for those less fortunate. For a few, it was a matter of personal survival causing them to make history-changing decisions or to rise above personal tragedy.

These women strongly believed in human rights, and their convictions empowered them to act. Stories of their behavior spread and influenced other women to break with tradition, often at personal risk. While their contributions to independence were cheered, the socioeconomic realities of their lives remained stagnant.[6]

Sometimes historical events masked the motives triggering the actions of these women who broke with tradition, and we are left wondering or guessing or making assumptions for their deeds. Did they reach out because to do so was less painful than to accept the existing situation? Were they gifted with independent natures, natural righters of wrongs? What personal wellspring did each tap to stretch higher and dig deeper into their souls, to defy authority and brave the world?

Information came from personal papers and first-hand reports. There were also legends passed down through the years. At times opinion clouded facts and fantasy eclipsed reality. There were misinterpretations and contradictions because of language, enthusiasm, and the passage of time, which colors memory. However, the message of their lives rings true: each woman was heroic.

Not all these women, a small sampling of many courageous Hispanic women, were born in Mexico or remained there. One arrived as a slave from another part of the world. Two were remembered for heroic deeds in the territory that became the State of Texas.

Many flames of courage shimmered brightly in the dark moments of history to join the glow of Doña Marina, Catarina de San Juan, Sor Juana, María Josefa, Leona

Vicario, Madam Candelaria, Francisco Alvarez, and Margarita Juárez. Together they were a sun shining gloriously on Mexico and reflecting on all of North America.

NOTES ON INTRODUCTION

1. Colin M. MacLachlan and Jaime E. Rodriguez O., *The Forging of the Cosmic Race: A Reinterpretation of Colonial Mexico* (Berkeley, Los Angeles, London: University of California Press, 1980), 229.
2. Ibid., 236, 237.
3. Ibid., 230-231.
4. John A. Crow, *The Epic of Latin America, Revised Edition* (Garden City, New York: Doubleday & Company, Inc., 1971), 280.
5. Charles Allen Smart, *Viva Juárez!* (Philadelphia: Lippincott, 1963), 406, and MacLachlan and Rodriguez O., *The Forging of the Cosmic Race: A Reinterpretation of Colonial Mexico*, 239.
6. Martha Cotera, *Profile on the Mexican American Woman* (Austin, Texas: National Education Laboratory Publishers, Inc., 1976), 36, 40; and Elizabeth Salas, *Soldaderas in the Mexican Military: Myth and History* (Austin: University of Texas Press, 1990), 28.

CHAPTER ONE

Doña Marina
Emancipator or Traitor?

No history of the conquest of Mexico is complete without considering the role played by Doña Marina, the young Indian princess who, by electing to assist the enemy of her country, became the most powerful woman in New Spain. She lived an almost legendary life, which makes her story, one of love and betrayal, all the more fascinating for its truth. Although there are countless variations to the tale, and as many uncertainties, the basic facts remain irrefutable.

To better understand what caused this woman to forsake her own people in order to further the cause of the Spanish *conquistador* Hernán Cortés, it is necessary to begin with her birth. She was born around the turn of the sixteenth century in Painala, a village in the region of Coatzacoalcos in southern Mexico. Her father, a rich and powerful Indian *cacique*, ruled as feudal lord over the natives living in the principal town of Painala and in the smaller agricultural districts surrounding their home.[1] At that time, with such notable exceptions as Tenochtitlán, Texcoco, Tlaxcala, and Cholula, Mexico was a country of moderate-sized villages. These were often dissimilar in dialect, dress, religious practices, and cultural heritage.[2] Her mother, said to be a ruler of a small nearby area called Xaltipan, was a handsome woman and apparently passed this attribute to her daughter. Firsthand reports of the girl by the *conquistadores* noted her attractiveness and the remarkable resemblance to her mother.[3]

In Aztec Mexico, families greeted news of pregnancy, particularly the first, with pleasure. They celebrated every birth and gathered with friends and neighbors to commemorate the naming of the child. Girls as well as boys were cherished. The midwife who delivered the child performed various naming rites, which included washing the baby and reciting prayers to ward off evil spirits. Symbols of household duties were shown to a girl and her umbilical cord was buried inside the home to indicate her proper place in life. For a boy, the symbols reflected battle or the trade he would follow; his umbilical cord was buried outside the home.[4]

To honor the birth of this girl, his firstborn child, the *cacique* may have planned a grand feast, while Indians under his vassalage hurried from nearby villages to pay homage with suitable gifts. Trinkets of gold, beautifully embroidered cotton cloth, grains, and exotic foods would insure her a happy life and gain favor from her father.

She was called Malinali or a variation of that. Perhaps she was named for the sign or date of her birth corresponding to the twelfth day of the month in the 365-day Nahua calendar or a similar measure of time. In the Sacred Almanac used by the priests to foretell the future, the word *malinalli* was represented by the hieroglyph or sign of twisted grass. There are a few references to a last name of Tenepal, a word thought to mean an animated and loquacious speaker, but such an appellation may have been awarded to describe her emerging personality, strong character, or even a family trait.[5]

All infants received the same care until weaned at age two or three, then instruction became the province of the same-sexed parent who began teaching by example. The education and training of daughters, including passing on the traditions and customs of each village, began in earnest at age five. Cooking, sewing, and embroidering were necessary skills for life in the community. A girl quickly learned the importance of proper behavior. She sat with her legs tucked modestly under her skirt; she never spoke disrespectfully to her parents or relatives; she avoided strangers, obeyed laws, and shunned evil. Children were expected to heed these lessons, and a prick with a cactus

Doña Marina

From Antigüedades mexicanas, *"Lienzo de Tlaxcala," Doña Marina at the left side of Cortés. Courtesy of the Nettie Lee Benson Latin American Collection, The General Libraries, The University of Texas at Austin.*

spine was enough punishment for any lazy or disobedient youngster.[6]

Presumably, Malinali spent a comfortable and un-eventful early childhood until the death, from an undisclosed cause, of her father. Soon after, her widowed mother remarried a younger man, also a *cacique*, and within a year gave birth to a son. Initially, her new stepfa-ther may have claimed to love the little girl as his own; however, the birth of his son drastically altered the situ-ation. Now Malinali's mother and stepfather wanted their newborn son to inherit the lands that according to Indian law rightfully belonged to the girl. Indeed, she later told the Spaniards she possessed both vassals and land. This was probably true as women in some Nahua towns, when in the direct line of succession, had the power to govern their own lands and were respected and obeyed as rulers.[7]

Secretly, the parents gave or sold the girl to a wander-ing tribe of Indian traders from Xicalango. That same night a child belonging to one of their Indian slaves coin-cidentally died or, more likely, was murdered as part of their plot. This girl, of approximately Malinali's age, was quickly buried before the dawn of the following day.[8] In the morning, the parents, exhibiting great sorrow and lamenting their loss with barely coherent utterances, told the villagers how the little girl died of a contagious fever during the night. They explained that they hastened to bury her before the disease could spread. No one dared to question this. Having no idea of her true identity or worth, the slave-traders eventually sold the bewildered and terrified child to a Tabascan chieftain of Potonchan, a hundred miles to the west of Coatzacoalcos. Her age at this time is unknown, but she was probably old enough to be aware of the complicity of her mother and stepfather in her abduction.[9]

Life for any slave was difficult, especially for a child raised as a princess. Chores once done by the slaves in her own village were now hers to do. She spent long hours kneeling over a metate grinding maize or cocoa and stood at a hot cooking fire stirring pots of beans and chilies to feed her master's family. She wove cotton and coarse maguey fiber into cloth and embroidered garments with the fine stitches learned at her mother's knee. With countless small children to watch over and the master's wife to obey, little time remained for rest from the grim reality of everyday existence. Slaves knew better than to attract attention by expressing displeasure in either word or deed; they lived in constant fear. Not only did their masters physically abuse them at times, but the ruthless emperor Montezuma II demanded human tribute for sacrifice to appease the insatiable Aztec gods. No slave, particularly if taken in tribal conflict, was safe from this butchery, no matter how clever or comely. Even infants and children were expendable; their tears before death, symbols of falling rain, were valuable offerings to the god responsible for growing crops.[10]

Several years passed as Malinali grew into young womanhood, uncertain of her future. Neither her beauty nor intelligence spared her from maltreatment. Drawing on the lessons of discipline and respect taught during her early childhood, she was submissive and obedient, suffering without complaint. She never forgot she was the daughter of a great chieftain, yet wisely kept her bitterness within. Malinali the child gave up hoping for her mother to rescue her until at last Malinali the young woman resigned herself to a life without hope, passing dispassionately through each day, unmoved by joy or grief.

Then, once again, fate intervened in the predictability of her life as Malinali became a chance participant in an event that changed the course of history and her life as well: the arrival of the *conquistador* Hernán Cortés.

Sailing with eleven ships and 550 men from Cuba on February 10, 1519, to claim Mexico in the name of his sovereign, Charles V of Spain, Cortés headed toward Cozumel. Two hundred Cuban natives acting as servants, sixteen horses, and several large hunting dogs accompanied the Spaniards. A well-organized, methodical planner, Cortés foresaw an orderly landing and exploration of the country, but from the beginning his plans went awry. Storms beleaguered the ships resulting in the loss of one, and the vessel in which Cortés sailed was blown off course. Now instead of his anticipated triumphant arrival at the head of his fleet, he found himself lagging at its rear.[11]

More problems greeted Cortés upon arrival. Pedro de Alvarado, captain of one of the first ships to land, had assumed command in Cortés' absence. He succeeded in driving away the local inhabitants, then sacked their village. An angry Cortés needed to undo the damage caused by the raid and entice the natives to return to their homes, which they had abandoned in fear of the approaching Spaniards.[12]

His first stroke of luck came unexpectedly from an Indian of Yucatán who had been taken prisoner and brought back to Cuba after an expedition by Hernández de Córdoba. The Indian, christened Melchorejo (Melchior) by the Spaniards, knew a few words of Spanish and acted as their interpreter. After speaking with the natives, he brought news of some Spaniards shipwrecked on an earlier expedition who were now living as slaves in a remote area not far from the coast. Cortés sent word by Indian traders that he wished to speak to these men. A few days later Jerónimo de Aguilar, looking more like a native than a Spaniard, arrived at their camp.[13]

Bernal Díaz del Castillo, a common foot soldier with Cortés, dictated a chronicle of the events of the conquest when he was eighty-four years old, blind, and hard of hearing. He described Aguilar's appearance as he approached through the brush carrying a paddle over his shoulder. The man was naturally brown and wore his hair shorn as an Indian slave. He was covered by a ragged cloak and a tattered loincloth; an old sandal dangled on one foot, its mate tied at his waist. Aguilar carried, wrapped in a bundle under his cloak, a much-used prayer book, the "Book of Hours."[14]

Aguilar, a Spaniard from Écija in Andalusia, on a holy mission to Santo Domingo, had been shipwrecked eight years earlier off the coast of Yucatán and held captive by the Indians of Catoche. There were seventeen survivors of the wreck, including two women. His voice, strained by the unaccustomed use of Spanish, was halting and at times laced with a strange vocabulary. He revealed that all were dead except for himself and Gonzalo Guerrero. With help from a friendly *cacique*, he and Guerrero escaped from cages in which they were kept to be fattened for sacrifice. Since then, Aguilar had labored as a common slave in the fields, cutting wood and carrying water. The *cacique* agreed to his release upon receiving the message, sweetened by a ransom of green beads, from Cortés. However, Guerrero, with his ears and nose pierced and his face and hands tattooed, was living well as a native. He chose to remain with his family: a wife and three children. Aguilar, whose Spanish rapidly returned as he spoke, was fluent in several local Mayan dialects and proved to be invaluable to Cortés.[15]

Cortés next sailed from Cozumel to the mouth of the Rio Grijalva located in the province of Tabasco. He expected a friendly welcome from the Tabascans, similar to that accorded an earlier expedition by Juan de Grijalva, but because they had been branded cowards by their neighbors after that reception, the Indians were prepared to make show of their courage. Massed along the marshy and uninviting shore, concealed from view by the evil-smelling mangrove swamps, they stood ready to defend their land from the white-faced, bearded intruders. Aguilar appealed for reason. He asked to come ashore for water and offered small tokens to trade for food. His pleas for friendship fell on ears deaf to all but their own shrill sounds. Amid a cacophony of blood-curdling screams, beating drums, and screeching conches, the Indians loosed a barrage of arrows, spears, and darts upon the Spaniards.

The Mexican Indians were brave warriors; they fought viciously, inflicting several wounds upon their foes, although, from the outset, there was little chance of victory against the well-trained Spanish troops. It was the appearance of soldiers on horseback that finally turned the tide of battle. The sudden charge by armor-clad cavaliers in plumed helmets, seated tall on what looked to be deer fitted with iron breastplates, their jangling bells a harbinger of death, took the fight out of the terrified Indians who had never seen such beasts. Imagining man and animal to be one and the same creature, they were convinced this was some vengeance-seeking god.[16]

The Tabascan chiefs soon came to discuss peace, offering small gold trinkets, foodstuffs, and cotton cloth, which Cortés graciously accepted while proffering his own gifts of blue and green glass beads. However, the most important gift from the lord of Potonchan was that of twenty slave girls to make tortillas and render other services for the Spaniards whom he noticed had no women of their own. This offering was more important than Cortés could have judged at the time and paved the way for his conquest of Mexico.

Among these slaves, mostly short and stocky, one stood out for her exceptional good looks, poise, and obvious intelligence. She was about nineteen years of age, slim, and slightly taller than the others, with a lighter complexion and finer features. She was called Malinali and baptized Marina, which probably sounded most like her own name to the Spaniards. These girls became the first Christian converts in New Spain, although it is doubtful that they had any choice in the matter. Cortés, thoroughly engrossed with his plans for conquest, did not take notice of these distinguishing qualities. Before awarding these girls to his captains, according to their rank and value to him, Cortés insisted they be baptized by Father Fray Bartolomé de Olmedo, who had accompanied him from Cuba. In this manner, Cortés could reconcile the adultery of the married soldiers as it was forbidden for the Spaniards to cohabit with native women not christened. Malinali was given to his most-favored soldier, Captain Alonso Hernández Portocarrero.[17]

The fleet then set sail for San Juan d Ulúa near Veracruz, arriving April 21, 1519, Holy Thursday. Cortés hoped to get further information from the natives using Jerónimo de Aguilar as interpreter, but this tongue was strange to Aguilar's ear. Cortés was furious. He needed to make himself understood to learn about this country and its ruler. At that moment, a voice came from the group of slave girls standing off to one side beneath the trees bordering the shoreline.[18]

"These men are Aztec. They speak Náhuatl." The voice of the newly christened slave Marina was clear and firm. She spoke calmly, courageously, as all heads turned toward her.

Undoubtedly, she bided her time, relying on her native instinct to watch and listen before speaking, assessing the consequences of such a bold action, weighing her options. Perhaps she believed Cortés was the Aztec god Quetzalcóatl, bearded and fair-skinned, returning as had been foretold. Possibly she determined that such a move might improve her lot as a slave. Although unaware of Cortés' plans when she seized this opportunity to call attention to herself, it was her first step toward freedom.

When she made the decision to assist the enemies of her people, she was already well grounded by a life of betrayal and adversity and thus felt no allegiance to her countrymen.

Speaking Maya, the language she learned as a slave, which Aguilar quickly translated into Spanish for Cortés, Marina proved to be the most valuable weapon in the Spanish arsenal. Aguilar translated Cortés' Spanish response into Maya and Marina changed the Maya into Náhuatl, the dominant language of Aztec Mexico, which she spoke as a child in Painala. Then this process was reversed. Later the time-consuming double translation became unnecessary as she quickly became fluent in Spanish and replaced Aguilar as chief translator.[19] By 1519, during the reign of Montezuma II, the Aztec empire encompassed almost thirty million people speaking a vast number of languages. It would have been impossible for Aguilar and Marina to understand more than a few dialects.[20]

Cortés, recognizing the girl's value and perhaps awakening to her charms, then took Marina away from his captain and to his own bed. When the Spaniards learned the story of her noble birth, they added the honorific Doña to her name to acknowledge her lineage and venerate her importance.[21] Her usefulness to Cortés lay not only in her ability to translate, but in that she was a shrewd judge of character. She advised him of how the Indians thought, warning him of hidden motives and treachery. She understood their native customs and habits, when to proceed cautiously without antagonizing them, when to show strength. Consequently, Cortés knew a great deal more about the Indians than they did about him.

Doña Marina also took advantage of their fears, religious beliefs, and superstitions to further Cortés' ambitions. She knew instinctively how to manipulate through political machination people already angered by tax gatherers and paying tribute in slaves. Her beguiling sincerity convinced captured Indians that Cortés would not harm them. Thus she easily gained their confidence and was able to supply him with information often confided to her in secret. More than once she saved the Spaniards from certain death.[22]

By August, Cortés, with Marina always at his side, pressed inland advancing on the Aztec capital city of Tenochtitlan through a succession of military engagements. The Mexicas (pronounced Mesheeca and the name used by the Aztecs to refer to themselves as a group) feared his arrival. They called Cortés "Marina's captain or Malinche." She was called "La Malinche." The name Malinche may have come from the mispronunciation of Malintzin. The Nahua suffix *tzin* added to Malinali showed respect. Cortés told her what to say, but it was Marina's inflection that delivered the message more clearly than his words. If she erred in translation, it did not impede the Spaniard's progress.[23]

Not far from his goal, Cortés counted on manipulating their fear and hatred to coerce the native Cholulans and Tlaxcalans to swell his army's ranks. However, en route to his long-anticipated confrontation with Montezuma, he sensed possible treachery. Acting on this, Marina charmed her way into the confidence of the wife of an Indian *cacique*. The woman admired her greatly, envisioning Doña Marina as a fine wife for her son, and suggested she might have valuable information for Cortés. Accepting an invitation to rest comfortably in the woman's home, Marina complained about her ill-treatment at the hands of the Spaniards. This pretext won the woman's trust and she revealed a Cholulan plot to attack Cortés.

The woman advised that some 20,000 Aztec warriors were gathering not far from the city where they planned to mount an attack when the Spaniards would be unprepared and easily defeated. Cortés immediately confirmed this information by questioning a Cholulan priest seized in order to corroborate this story. He was able to outsmart the enemy, killing thousands of natives and reaffirming the superiority of the Spaniards' might. In this way, Marina may have been indirectly responsible for the infamous slaughter in Cholula.[24]

Meanwhile, Montezuma awaited the arrival of the Cortés entourage with great apprehension. Who was this stranger? Was he a man? Was he Quetzalcóatl, the Feathered Serpent, White God of the Aztecs, or his representative returning from the Western seas? Montezuma was already weakened by superstition. For two years there had been omens presaging the coming of Cortés: floods, fires igniting for no reason, comets blazing across the skies, children born deformed.[25]

That a woman of their own race was bringing the intruders to him was of great concern. No matter their birthright, noble or common, females stayed at home tending children, cooking, weaving, caring for their men. Doña Marina's strong physical presence and the deference conferred upon her by Spaniards and Indians alike was an affront to the Aztec culture. Women had no voice in the patriarchal Aztec society, yet here she stood in his palace demanding that his nobles bring food and water for the strangers and their beasts. At first, the Mexicas stood as if frozen, afraid to obey, yet too intimidated by *La Malinche* and the Spaniards to refuse.[26] Whatever his fears, Montezuma graciously extended his hospitality to the Spaniards. Using the Indian name for Marina, he referred to her as Cortés' ambassador. He was relieved to hear her speaking Náhuatl, their native tongue. Although dressed no differently than any woman in his land, in a long wrap-around skirt covered by a simple *huipil*,[27] she held her head high like a princess and her voice rang strongly like a *cacica*.

Speaking through Marina, Cortés said they came as friends, and Montezuma welcomed them with an exhibition of wealth from his treasury. This bounty of gold further inflamed the Spaniards' greed, while articles made of quetzal feathers and jadeite, highly valued by the Mexicas, were of little interest. The objects shown to them earlier by the Indians along their route paled in the light of Montezuma's hoard. In the days that followed, Marina, accompanying Cortés and acting upon his directions, alternately cajoled and threatened Montezuma into submission. How accurate were her translations? Did she couch the *conquistador's* words in phrases more advantageous to herself or to put herself in a more powerful position? And was she able to correctly translate Montezuma's more formal language, which may have differed from her rough native dialect?[28]

For a time Cortés was willing to dally in a friendly relationship with Montezuma. He planned to use persuasion, not force, to subjugate Mexico and thought to induce Montezuma to voluntarily become his prisoner. Marina explained to the emperor that he would be treated with respect for his royal position. He could take with him his family, his several wives, their retainers, and all the material things necessary for his personal comfort. When at last Montezuma yielded, he was moved to his new quarters where, with the exception of the Spanish guards, everything appeared to be normal.[29]

Suddenly Cortés was forced to leave for Veracruz to deal with Spanish troops sent by the Cuban governor, Diego de Velázquez. The fleet of eighteen ships, sailing under the command of Pánfilo de Narváez, planned to take possession of the land Cortés conquered and arrest the ambitious *conquistador*, whom the Spanish authorities accused of overstepping his boundaries. In Cortés' absence, Pedro de Alvarado, left in charge at the capital city, became nervous when Aztec noblemen gathered to celebrate a religious rite. Fearing imminent attack, Alvarado struck first, killing many of the unarmed warriors and further inciting the hostile Mexicas. Cortés, after successfully avoiding capture, returned with an even larger army to face the threat of an uprising. In an effort to placate the Aztecs, the Spaniards ordered Montezuma to the roof of his courtyard prison to plead for peace. Mexicas, incensed by the emperor's acquiescence, let loose a barrage of stones, darts, and other missiles on the Spaniards standing with Montezuma in their midst. The emperor was wounded by a blow to the head from a stone thrown from the raging mob. He was taken below to his apartment, where he died as a direct result of this injury.[30]

In the ensuing battle, both sides suffered incredible losses. The Spaniards were forced to flee Tenochtitlan, but not without first removing what treasure they could carry. Cortés warned that the wisest manner of exit would be at night, carrying the lightest load. But the gold-hungry soldiers, who had suffered great hardship over the course of the conquest, refused to leave without their rightful due. In the end, it was this greed which caused their deaths by drowning or by sacrifice when captured. In all, four hundred and fifty Spaniards died that night. The slaughter that accompanied their retreat was one of the bloodiest in the history of New Spain and remembered in history as *la noche triste*, the sad night. As the survivors regrouped on the other side of the causeway, Cortés sat weeping beneath a large tree.[31]

Amazingly, Marina, in the safekeeping of a Tlaxcalan chief, escaped and reunited with Cortés. After their escape from the Mexicas, there is little mention of her role as interpreter in the conflicts that continued to besiege the Spaniards until their final triumph on August 13, 1521.[32] In the five letters he wrote to Charles V, Cortés made scant note of Marina, referring to her in his second letter merely as "a native Indian girl" given to him and acting as his interpreter, and again, in his fifth letter, he wrote of "the interpreter, Marina, who has ever accompanied me...." A vainglorious man, he gave little credit to the woman who stood at his side on his march to immortality.[33]

Whether he truly loved Marina as she did him is doubtful. Cortés had no intention of marrying her. He had a wife in Spain, Doña Catalina Suárez, and it would not be advisable for a man of his stature to bring home an Indian wife. It was no secret that he was an accomplished womanizer and had fathered several illegitimate children. While in Mexico, Cortés had several Indian mistresses, including daughters and a niece of Montezuma.[34] Marina knew of his numerous liaisons, but again wisely kept her own council. Certainly, he tired of her affections, possibly after she bore him one son in 1522, Martín, who later returned to Spain with Cortés and was said to have been his favorite.[35]

Then in 1523, while travelling through Coatzacoalcos on his way to Honduras, Cortés called a meeting with the local *caciques*. It was here that Marina came face to face with her mother and stepbrother, now baptized Marta and Lazarus, who jointly ruled over their territory. The resemblance between mother and daughter was remarkable and could not be denied. The pair fell to their knees in terror awaiting death. Marina, without question the most powerful woman in New Spain, reassured them by saying that when she became a Christian and gave up idol worship, she learned forgiveness. She pardoned her mother's sin, excusing it by saying the woman was ignorant of the consequences of her deed. Bernal Díaz del Castillo recalled that Marina gave them some of her own jewels and apparel and sent them away.[36]

During this expedition to Honduras, Cortés arranged a marriage between Marina and one of his soldiers, a cavalier named Juan Jaramillo, at the town of Orizaba. Their union produced one daughter, María. For her efforts on his behalf, Cortés gave Marina an estate at Jilotepec, a village fifty miles north of Mexico City. He later granted her additional land near Mexico City.[37] With resignation learned over a short but beleaguered lifetime, Marina accepted her fate. As a mature and practical woman, she knew Cortés would never return to her. As a native familiar with the ways of slavery and the traditional role of women, she knew her place.

Little more is known about the slave girl who rose to such prominence, and to this day, she remains a contradiction: at the same time revered and hated, savior or traitor.[38] To the Spaniards she was Doña Marina, a woman honored for her part in the conquest of Mexico. And as a native, she was sympathetic to the plight of the much abused Indians. Yet she betrayed her people and was responsible in great measure for the downfall of Montezuma and the Aztec nation.

Marina died in the middle of the sixteenth century. Her Indian appellation, *La Malinche*, became an epithet for traitor. Today, *malinchismo* is used as a word of reproach for a Mexican accused of being unpatriotic, and a person who prefers that which is foreign and rejects his national heritage is termed *malinchista*.[39]

Many legends surround the name of *La Malinche*. It is said her spirit watches over the capital she helped conquer, an apparition of an Indian princess appearing in the evening shadows, a strong presence among the groves and grottos of the royal Hill of Chapultepec. Her spirit also wanders in the woodland surrounding an ancient church in the village of Atzcapotzalco, about five miles from Mexico City, at the site of an early Chichimecas slave market. Her remorse allows her no peace. She is again seen near Tlaxcala as a deity of a mountain called the Dark Green Woman (Matlalcueyetl) and known as *La Malinche*.[40]

And some say she is *La Llorana*, a white ghost, crying in the night for the betrayal of her country, the loss of her son, and for the love of a man who was never hers.[41]

NOTES ON CHAPTER ONE

1. Bernal Díaz del Castillo, *The Discovery and Conquest of Mexico, 1517-1521* (London: George Routledge & Sons, Ltd., 1928), 115.

2. Michael C. Meyer and William L. Sherman, *The Course of Mexican History: Third Edition* (New York, Oxford: Oxford University Press, 1987), 82.

3. Díaz del Castillo, *The Discovery and Conquest of Mexico, 1517-1521*, 117; and Hugh Thomas, *Conquest: Montezuma, Cortés, and the Fall of Old Mexico* (New York, London, Toronto, Sydney, Tokyo, Singapore: Simon & Schuster, 1993), 172.

4. Frances F. Berdan, *Indians of North America: The Aztecs* (New York, Philadelphia: Chelsea House Publishers, 1989), 40, 63; Sonia Bleeker, *The Aztec Indians of Mexico,* (New York: William Morrow & Co., 1963), 38-39; Albert Marrin, *Aztecs and Spaniards: Cortes and the Conquest of Mexico* (New York: Atheneum, 1986), 29; and Martha Cotera, *Profile on the Mexican American Woman* (Austin, Texas: National Educational Laboratory Publishers, Inc., 1976), 16-17.

5. William Weber Johnson, *Cortés* (Boston, Toronto: Little, Brown and Company, 1975), 43; and Thomas, *Conquest: Montezuma, Cortés, and the Fall of Old Mexico,* 172.

6. Bleeker, *The Aztec Indians of Mexico*, 43-44; and Marrin, *Aztecs and Spaniards: Cortes and the Conquest of Mexico,* 30; and Meyer and Sherman, *The Course of Mexican History: Third Edition,* 77-78; and Cotera, *Profile on the Mexican American Woman,* 18-20.

7. Captain Bernal Díaz del Castillo, Translated from original Spanish by Maurice Keatinge, *The True History of the Conquest of Mexico* (New York: Robert M. McBride

& Company, 1927), 79; and Cotera, *Profile on The Mexican American Woman*, 21-23.

8. Díaz del Castillo, *The Discovery and Conquest of Mexico, 1517-1521*, 115-116; and Johnson, *Cortés*, 43.

9. Thomas, *Conquest: Montezuma, Cortés, and the Fall of Old Mexico*, 172; and Henry Morton Robinson, *Stout Cortez: A Biography of the Spanish Conquest* (New York: The Century Co., 1931), 65-66.

10. Marrin, *Aztecs and Spaniards: Cortes and the Conquest of Mexico*, 38-43; and Jonathan Kandell, *La Capital: The Biography of Mexico City* (New York: Random House, 1988), 60.

11. Marshall McClintock, *Prescott's The Conquest of Mexico, Designed for Modern Reading* (New York: Julian Messner, 1948), 18; and Meyer and Sherman, *The Course of Mexican History: Third Edition*, 101; and Thomas, *Conquest: Montezuma, Cortés, and the Fall of Old Mexico*, 158.

12. Beatrice Berler, *The Conquest of Mexico: A Modern Rendering of William H. Prescott's History* (San Antonio: Corona Publishing Company, 1988), 14.

13. Miguel Leon-Portilla, *Broken Spears: The Aztec Account of the Conquest of Mexico* (Boston: Beacon Press, 1962), 31; and Kandell, *La Capital: The Biography of Mexico City*, 95-96.

14. Albert Idell, tr. and ed., *The Bernal Díaz Chronicles: The True Story of the Conquest of Mexico* (Garden City, New York: Doubleday & Company, 1957), 42.

15. Ibid., 42; and Thomas, *Conquest: Montezuma, Cortés, and the Fall of Old Mexico*, 163-164.

16. Berler, *The Conquest of Mexico: A Modern Rendering of William H. Prescott's History*, 16-17; and Thomas, *Conquest: Montezuma, Cortés, and the Fall of Old Mexico*, 165-167; and McClintock, *Prescott's The Conquest of Mexico, Designed for Modern Reading*, 22-24.

17. Johnson, *Cortés*, 42-44; and Jerome R. Adams, *Liberators and Patriots of Latin America: Biographies of 23 Leaders from Doña Marina (1505-1530) to Bishop Romero (1917-1980)* (Jefferson, North Carolina, and London: McFarland & Company, Inc., 1991), 4-5; and Thomas, *Conquest: Montezuma, Cortés, and the Fall of Old Mexico*, 172.

18. Meyer and Sherman, *The Course of Mexican History: Third Edition*, 102; and Francisco López de Gómara, *Cortés, The Life of the Conqueror by His Secretary*. Lesley Byrd Simpson, tr. and ed., from the "Istoria de la Conquista de Mexico," Zaragoza, 1552 (Berkeley: University of California Press, 1964), 56.

19. Adams, *Liberators and Patriots of Latin America: Biographies of 23 Leaders*, 3.

20. Meyer and Sherman, *The Course of Mexican History: Third Edition*, 89; and Michael D. Coe, *Ancient Peoples and Places: Mexico* (New York: Frederick A. Praeger, Publisher, 1962), 28.

21. Marrin, *Aztecs and Spaniards: Cortes and the Conquest of Mexico*, 77.

22. Adams, *Liberators and Patriots of Latin America: Biographies of 23 Leaders*, 2; and Johnson, *Cortés*, 44; and Díaz del Castillo, *The Discovery and Conquest of Mexico, 1517-1521*, 115.

23. Thomas, *Conquest: Montezuma, Cortés, and the Fall of Old Mexico*, 172; and *Enciclopedia de México, Tomo VIII* (Ciudad de México, S.A.: Instituto de la Enciclopedia de México, 1974), 233.

24. Johnson, *Cortés*, 93; and Meyer and Sherman, *The Course of Mexican History: Third Edition*, 109; and T.R. Fehrenbach, *Fire and Blood: A History of Mexico* (New York: Macmillan Publishing Co., Inc., 1973), 131-132.

25. Kandell, *La Capital: The Biography of Mexico City*, 68-69; and Thomas, *Conquest: Montezuma, Cortés, and the Fall of Old Mexico*, 41.

26. Ibid., 173, 285, 296; and Leon-Portilla, *Broken Spears: The Aztec Account of the Conquest of Mexico*, 69.

27. Bleeker, *The Aztec Indians of Mexico*, 21.

28. Leon-Portilla, *Broken Spears: The Aztec Account of the Conquest of Mexico*, 68; and Thomas, *Conquest: Montezuma, Cortés, and the Fall of Old Mexico*, 279, 296.

29. McClintock, *Prescott's The Conquest of Mexico, Designed for Modern Reading*, 153-154.

30. Marrin, *Aztecs and Spaniards: Cortes and the Conquest of Mexico*, 120-128; and Thomas, *Conquest: Montezuma, Cortés, and the Fall of Old Mexico*, 383-402; and Johnson, *Cortés*, 126.

31. Thomas, *Conquest: Montezuma, Cortés, and the Fall of Old Mexico*, 409-412; and Meyer and Sherman, *The Course of Mexican History: Third Edition*, 120-124.

32. Adams, *Liberators and Patriots of Latin America: Biographies of 23 Leaders*, 11; and McClintock, *Prescott's The Conquest of Mexico, Designed for Modern Reading*, 228.

33. Sir E. Denison Ross and Eileen Power, eds., and F. Bayard Morris, tr., *Hernando Cortés: Five Letters, 1519-1526* (London: George Routledge & Sons, Ltd., 1928), 57, 313.

34. Thomas, *Conquest: Montezuma, Cortés, and the Fall of Old Mexico*, 313.

35. Ibid., 580.

36. Díaz del Castillo, Keatinge, tr., *The True History of the Conquest of Mexico*, 79-80.

37. Adams, *Liberators and Patriots of Latin America: Biographies of 23 Leaders*, 12.

38. Fehrenbach, *Fire and Blood: A History of Mexico*, 131.

39. Johnson, *Cortés*, 222.

40. *Enciclopedia de México, Tomo VIII*, 233-234; and Bernice I. Goodspeed, *Mexican Tales* (Mexico, D.F.: American Book & Printing Co., S.A., 1946), 181-182; and Maurice Collis, *Cortés and Montezuma* (London: Faber and Faber, mcmliv), 233, 235.

41. Adams, *Liberators and Patriots of Latin America: Biographies of 23 Leaders*, 12.

CHAPTER TWO

Catarina de San Juan
The Legend of la China Poblana

The sun was high as the *Manila Galleon* lowered its sails in the ancient port of Acapulco in 1621. Traders and merchants from Puebla de los Angeles, Veracruz, and Mexico City competed for space at the crowded wharf. They would remain until their purses of silver were exchanged for the rich cargo on board. The ship carried precious pearls and perfumes, spices and incense. There were luxurious silks, damask, velvets, all in great demand by the women of New Spain who arrived in increasing numbers each year from the Old World. Fine woods from Sumatra and the Malay Peninsula, gold and silver ornaments from Macao, shawls from Manila, and folding screens of red lacquer from the Orient filled its hold. Religious icons made of ivory and decorative porcelain tableware were packed in barrels and lashed to the decks. The *Manila Galleon* also brought slaves.[1]

Catarina de San Juan came to New Spain as a slave on this ship. She was born early in the seventeenth century somewhere in the Mughal Empire of India. Her name then was Myrrha, a word she defined as bitterness. When Myrrha was ten years old, she fled the city of her birth with her privileged family to escape from war and found refuge on the west coast of India in a harbor town ruled by the Portuguese. However, this location on the Arabian Sea was not without danger. Heavy commerce along the Malabar coast nearby attracted bands of pirates who sailed the coastal waters preying upon small merchant ships and making occasional forays into seaside villages.[2]

One day, while playing with a younger brother at the sandy beach adjacent to their home, Myrrha strayed too far from her servant and was kidnapped by marauding Portuguese pirates. She was taken to their ship and, once aboard, stripped of her gold ornaments and her sari woven of fine cotton, and given a sack-like garment of inferior goods to cover her nakedness. Deaf to her cries, the pirate captain slung her below decks to join other captives bound for the slave market in Manila.

As the ship sailed from the port of her abduction, the pirates decided to gamble Myrrha's fate with a game of cards—the winner to possess the girl. Their game erupted into a fight, until one declared that it would be better that she die than all of them. So saying, he threw a javelin at the child, wounding her in the thigh. Although one pirate hastened to her aid, none tried to claim her as his own.[3]

Myrrha huddled in pain on the floor of the creaking vessel, confused by the strange dialects assailing her ears. No hand reached out to help her. The stench from unwashed bodies lying in their own filth made her retch. She sickened from the motion of the ship and subsisted on scraps of rancid food when she could eat at all. She no longer cried.

The ship sailed south along the Malabar coast and landed at Cochin on the southern tip of India. During a lengthy stay in this port, Myrrha received religious

Catarina de San Juan

Dated 1688. From Catarina de San Juan, princesa de la India y visionaria de Puebla. *Courtesy of the Nettie Lee Benson Latin American Collection, The General Libraries, The University of Texas at Austin.*

instruction from a resident Jesuit priest and was baptized Catarina de San Juan. The Jesuits lived for many years in Cochin seeking conversions by preaching the gospel to sailors and slaves alike. Myrrha's spiritual nature made her a ready convert, and following the sacrament-of-baptism ceremony, she saw the Virgin holding the baby Jesus. She later told her confessor, Alonso Ramos, that they called out to her, and the intensity of this vision left her passionately committed to the Child. Ramos later took every opportunity to compare the events of Catarina's life with Jesus and other Catholic or biblical figures.

When the pirates landed in Manila, the captives were taken to the slave market. It was Holy Friday and Catarina witnessed a procession of penitents carrying crosses on their shoulders depicting Christ's crucifixion. She saw in the image of Jesus the picture of her own father and understood this to be another sign to deepen her belief.[4]

The slave market in Manila teemed with inhumanity. The air was rank from countless bodies awash in sweat and fear. Brawny men and lean boys, not quite men, their black and brown and yellow skins shimmering in the heat, strained at chains or ropes. Women clutching babies to their breasts and nubile girls cowered in the chaos. With eyes ablaze in hatred or dulled from starvation and lashings, they looked out at those wrangling over their bodies like animals being chosen for slaughter.

One of those interested in buying a slave that day was the captain of the *Manila Galleon*. He had been commissioned by Don Miguel de Sosa, a prosperous resident of Puebla, a city in New Spain, to purchase a *china* to care for the man's ailing wife. Catarina's large black eyes, which mirrored the innocence of the unfortunate child, captured his attention. He felt compelled to buy her. He knew de Sosa and his wife would shelter her from additional harm. Catarina's fragile beauty also attracted the eye of an agent representing a viceroy from Mexico. Don Diego Carrillo, *marquéz de los Gélves*, a Spaniard living in Acapulco, had ordered a pretty young girl to serve in his household. The captain, acting quickly, bid ten times more for the girl than the agent and hurriedly dressed her as a boy in order to keep her identity hidden from the viceroy of Puebla. Then he took her to his ship.[5]

The *Manila Galleon* was one of two ships crossing the Pacific between the Philippines and Acapulco each year. In 1565 these ships, manned by seamen from Portugal and Spain, began making once-a-year round trips to transport treasures from the East. Among its typical passengers were solitary noblemen, merchants from China and the Philippines, priests from the order of St. Augustine, and families seeking new vistas. Although these crossings were advertised to take seven months, a longer passage was likely if the seas were rough and storms blew the vessel off course. A lengthier voyage exposed travelers to disease caused by the lack of pure water, fresh food, and vermin, and were not for the fainthearted.[6]

As the ship maneuvered close to the dock in Acapulco, Catarina gazed out at the sea and up at the clouds as if searching for guidance. From the little Spanish she learned during the long months at sea, she understood that this was now her home and someone was waiting for her. Meanwhile, Don de Sosa, waiting in the heat, was impatient to see the slave bought at his behest. At last, the captain pointed to the sad-eyed child dressed as a boy. She was perched on a coil of rope near the bales of silk.

De Sosa appeared pleased with the gentle manner of the child. When informed of her baptism, he decided to have her confirmed in the Catholic faith as soon as possible, acting as her godparent. However, he did not regard her as his child or set her free. Nevertheless, Catarina, with memories of her own happy family, was thankful to be part of their home and for their protection.

Many legends connect this child, Catarina de San Juan, with one of the traditional female costumes of Mexico: *la china poblana*. The comparison may stem from a confusion in terms. In seventeenth-century Mexico, *la china* referred to a female maid or servant. Therefore, the word may reflect an occupation rather than ethnic makeup.

Filipinos particularly fell into this category. People of New Spain requested *chinas* from the Philippines because these girls were known to be honest, clean, and eager to help. Furthermore, they were loyal, rarely ran away, and served their masters as respectfully as they would their own parents. This was one reason for the popularity of the slave market in Manila.

Chino described anyone coming from the East, no matter skin color or the shape of the eyes. It could mean an offspring of any mixed union of Indian, black, mulatto, Spanish, or Oriental. The word *poblana* did not necessarily point to a native of the city of Puebla, but suggested a female belonging to any village.[7]

Catarina was an obedient and loyal servant, lavishing tender care upon de Sosa's wife, Doña Margarita de Chávez. She proved to be a skillful cook and chocolate maker, and even prepared the host for the Jesuits. In time de Sosa gave her control of the household budget and found she was neither extravagant nor penurious. Her work as a seamstress and her fine embroidery earned praise, and soon she became a familiar presence in the unpaved streets of Puebla. When not needed in the de Sosa home, she cared for sick and indigent *poblanos*, and word of her miraculous curative powers began to spread among the Spanish, Indian, and mestizo populace.

De Sosa urged Catarina to learn to read and write, but this seemed beyond her capabilities. To make herself understood in writing, she resorted to hieroglyphics. Her inability to read was seen as divine intervention as she believed all she needed to know came from the highest power. She could talk for hours and never tire, yet was incapable of speaking Spanish correctly. Her words came from God, she insisted, but others saw her as a poor uneducated slave. Once, to test her honesty, her confessor offered her a peso for no ostensible reason. Catarina recognized his motive and heatedly protested. She insisted she was an honest woman, not a liar, and that noble blood ran through her veins, even though she lived as a slave.[8]

Catarina, a devout Catholic, spent many hours in the church with her confessors who became her earliest biographers. She told them of her talks with Jesus Christ, the Virgin Mary, angels, saints, the deceased, and even demons. However, this material, used in their stories and based on the tales from her childhood and her spiritual visions, was clouded by their own interpretation and subjectivity. These works of her confessors painted a confusing and fanciful picture of the woman.

El Sermón was published by the Jesuit Francisco de Aguilera on January 24, 1688, at the time of her funeral in Puebla. It extolled the virtues of her life and spoke of her religious visions. Aguilera, coming from Mexico City, became a Jesuit in 1670 and taught language, philosophy, and theology. When not teaching, he preached to the neighboring Indians. The Jesuits established themselves in New Spain in 1572, committed to the education of the natives and the whites.

Alonso Ramos, also a Jesuit, was born in the town of Santa Eulalia and became a rector of the *colegio del Espíritu Santo* in Puebla and the *Profesa* in Mexico City. A learned man and prolific writer, he wrote several versions of her *vida*. Three volumes of her life were published in 1689, 1690, and 1692. Ramos exaggerated Catarina's virtues, as well as the spiritual aspects of her life, in his quest to have her declared a saint.

Another cleric, José del Castillo Graxeda, provided a third source of information. In his *Compendio* of 1692, he said there were many persons who did not hold with the assertions of saintliness made by Ramos. Graxeda, an excellent writer and respected anthologist, was the most realistic of Catarina's early biographers and tempered the excesses of Ramos. He understood how difficult it would be to verify the incidents of her life.[9]

Catarina said her mother's name was Borda and her grandfather was called Maxim. She forgot her father's name, but thought he was a prince of Arabia and India. From this scant information it was impossible to trace her roots. However, there were events from early childhood she related in great detail, and these were glorified by Ramos who found theological comparisons in most incidents.

She believed the Virgin attended her birth and recalled a fall from her crib when she was two years old. She crawled to a river and a woman took her from the water, somewhat in the manner of Moses. At the age of six, a Hindu holy man frightened Catarina with a prophecy of marriage. To escape his words, she ran into a cave of serpents, but emerged unharmed.[10]

A noble Hindu in Cochin rescued her from the pirates, although how he managed this was not explained, and brought her to his home to be educated and prepared for marriage. A young woman living in the house became jealous of Catarina's beauty and tortured her. She was dragged across the floor, tied uncomfortably for hours, and left for days without food. Her face was scratched, her hair was pulled and set on fire. Finally, desperate to be rid of Catarina, the woman tied a heavy stone to her chest and threw her into the sea. Catarina credited God for saving her because she fell close to the anchor of a ship and pulled herself to the surface. A Portuguese dock worker took her from the water and returned her to the pirates.

Did these events actually occur or were they the rambling of a lonely young woman given to asceticism in an age of religious fervor? Perhaps the Jesuits were too eager to discover miracles for the glorification of the Church.[11]

Catarina viewed herself as one unworthy of God's love and sought to attain a higher moral level by practicing self-denial and self-mortification. In this, she emulated nuns from the convent in Puebla who, like others of that period, were extreme in these practices. She may have found encouragement for this personal abasement from her confessors. Reports of miracles and visions were widely acknowledged by church seniors. The Spanish Inquisition was not as accepting and often these visionaries were condemned as heretics.

De Sosa often discovered her shedding uncontrollable tears from mystical feelings. He would find her in a small secret hiding place, kneeling with outstretched arms, and praying as if her heart burned with divine fire. Food did not interest her. When she slept, it was on the floor. De Sosa ordered her to eat and sleep.[12]

When Don Miguel de Sosa died on December 4, 1624, his will granted freedom to his slave with the condition that she continue as a servant to Doña Margarita. He left no money to Catarina, which showed he never considered her a real daughter. When Doña Margarita retired to the convent of Santa Teresa, Catarina was left without a home. Pedro Suárez, a cleric, came to her aid and gave her a room in his house. He also had a slave, a *chino*, named Domingo Suárez. Domingo fell in love with Catarina, but frightened her with his marriage proposal. She repeatedly ignored him, and when he persisted she informed him of her vow of chastity, which was her personal decision and not decreed by the church.

In 1626, to placate Domingo, she consulted her confessor and then consented to marry, but refused to lie with him. Although Domingo promised to respect her vow, he was furious when she would not meet her marital obligation. Catarina hung a crucifix between their beds to preserve her virginity and protect herself from Domingo's harassment. She was now about seventeen years of age, and her physical appearance noticeably changed. Her once delicate skin became dry, her hair lost its luster, her expression saddened, and she seemed to age. She had stopped eating, which affected her health and brought on a haggard look.

Domingo was a jealous man, and irrespective of her vow of chastity he feared other alliances. He insisted she move to the convent of Santa Teresa where he worked as a servant. His wife's refusal to share his bed finally drove Domingo to an affair with a poor woman, and he brought the children from this union to Catarina for care. It was not uncommon for married men to maintain second households while their wives looked the other way.[13] It was unlikely that Catarina had the strength or means to raise these children. Domingo left Puebla to work and live in Veracruz where he engaged in several unsuccessful business ventures. When he died in 1644, Catarina admitted feeling both physical and spiritual relief. At this time, Captain Hipólito del Castillo y Altra offered her shelter in his house near *la iglesia de la Compañía*.

There appears to be no connection between this pious woman of the seventeenth century who lived an almost monastic life and the festive costume: *la china poblana*. With the exception of her shawl, draped like an Indian sari, nothing in her attire inspired reverence through mimicry or influenced the style of the women of Puebla. Even before her time in Puebla, *rebozos* were used by women and girls to carry babies or to bundle their wares. If legend confused her with more self-reliant *chinas* of a different age, how did the legend begin?[14]

The poor woman's dress did not resemble the *china poblana* or any of the festive costumes of Mexico. Her attire was more like that of a nun or a servant. A dark skirt, worn over an underskirt of plain cloth, touched the floor; a closed jerkin of brown or black, sleeves tight around the arms, reached below her wrists; her underwear was the coarsest cotton. She covered her head with a white wrap made of cheap goods. It was fastened by a pin and worn like a veil to conceal her face. Catarina wanted to dress as a man and serve as a Jesuit priest because she believed these men ascended directly to heaven.[15]

In 1625 a Dominican priest, Thomas Gage, described the dress of native black or mulatto women. Their long full skirts were stitched with gold or silver thread, worn with embroidered low-cut white blouses, and covered by mantillas of linen or chambray. This was before, according to legend, her memory was honored by the women of Puebla. Later, women of different castes working as maids, cooks, and fresh water vendors wore similar costumes. Their colorful skirts, white décolleté blouses, and *rebozos* created a festive parade along the dusty streets.[16] Today, according to the indigenous group wearing it and the particular festive occasion, the costume appears in a myriad of fabrics and decorations. The colors red, white, and green most often worn represent the Mexican flag.[17]

Catarina became the heroine of many charming stories. In one version an English pirate abducted her from a Chinese boat to steal her fine possessions. He sold her to a merchant who, in turn, sold her as a slave to de Sosa. The kindly citizen of Puebla freed the girl, replaced her rich wardrobe, and put her in the safekeeping of a convent to be educated. Catarina then sold her finery to buy clothes for poor children and, in the winter, covered her simple red full skirt, plain shirt, and *rebozo* with a goatskin coat. Her beguiling costume was adopted by maid servants in the convent.

In one story Myrrha, a Hindu princess born in 1609, was stolen by a Portuguese ship owner, a pirate in disguise. The family had escaped to an unnamed seaport when the Turks attacked her father's kingdom in India. Don de Sosa's quick actions at the moment of her sale saved her from the viceroy.[18] Another tale had Catarina remaking her original elegant clothes using regional fabrics and the women of Puebla adopting the fashion of her Indian sari out of devotion to the saintly woman.

Each account verified that she was kidnapped, came as a slave to Mexico, lived with de Sosa, and married *"con separación de lechos,"* with separate beds.[19]

Like many religious persons, Catarina felt unworthy of God's favor and feared heaven's gate would be closed to her. The austerities of her life, the denial and self-mortification, were attempts to purify her soul. At times she described her visions as dreams and her physical pain as imaginary. Her doctor, Juan de Torres Guevara, revealed that from the time Catarina reached the age of seventy, she felt intense cold from her waist to her feet. This prevented movement for hours; the numbness caused agonizing pain. Above her waist she was flushed with searing heat, a sensation which passed in a day, leaving her feeling fine. At times she itched as if she suffered from mange or herpes, but her doctor found no cause for this. Then she broke her arm in a fall and lost control of her bodily functions. A paralyzing stroke followed.

Catarina saw her prayers mounting to heaven as wisps of clouds and their answers came as flowers in a garden. She faced the torments in her life as predestinated by God and suffered the mockery of children and ridicule of adults humbly,[20] living as an autistic in a world of her own making.

She continued to speak of religious visions until her death at the age of eighty-two. In her final dream she heard voices telling of the honors she would receive at her funeral, which were God's will. She saw the bishop of Puebla walking in the long procession of mourners and heard the bells of the city tolling her passing. Ramos took advantage of that dream, describing it as if it were real. However, the bishop was not in the city. Preceding her death at four in the morning on January 5, 1688, a bright light appeared in the sky.

No tears fell during the ritual preceding interment: no one cries at the burial of a saint. Her shroud was a black robe resembling the garb of the Jesuits. Was this again providential, as Ramos claimed, or a mistake of the tailor? Purple silk covered the open coffin to honor her nobility, and for two days people came to visit, kiss her still form, and take pieces of her robe. A procession of councilmen, clerics, knights of military orders, and a choir of boys accompanied the coffin, which was carried by the mayor and city officials. The coffin was closed for the last time and covered with a black cloth.

In 1691 the Inquisition prohibited the circulation of Catarina's portrait, both the one of her alone and the one in which she appeared in the company of Bishop Juan Palafox y Mendoza. Eight years after her death, the Inquisition also banned books written about her life citing the abuse of theological comparison and the exaggeration of her virtues made by her biographers.[21]

Catarina de San Juan was forgotten by history. The mystery of her connection with the flamboyant national folk costume of Mexico was never solved. Yet the legends passed from mother to daughter, crossing generations. For many, she will always be *la china poblana*, the lovely child, brutally kidnapped and condemned to a life as a slave, who courageously, and without complaint, dedicated her life to helping others.

NOTES ON CHAPTER TWO

1. Francisco de la Maza, *Catarina de San Juan: princesa de la India y visionaria de Puebla*, Elisa Vargaslugo, prologo. Cien de Mexico. (Mexico, D.F.: Consejo Nacional para la Cultura y las Artes, Dirección General de Comunicaciones, 1990), 14, 21. The date of Catarina's arrival varies, even in the same source, on page 14, "at the end of the year 1621," and on page 21, "May 1621." Other sources have her arrival in 1620 or as late as 1625.

2. Ibid., 14, 21, 37 (The spelling of her name differs according to the source.), 40; and W.H. Moreland and Atul Chandra Chatterjee, *A Short History of India: Fourth Edition* (New York: David McKay Company, Inc., 1957), 200-202.

3. Maza, *Catarina de San Juan: princesa de la India y visionaria de Puebla*, 40.

4. Ibid., 41-42. This is also attributed to Ramos.

5. Ibid., 22, 42.

6. Ibid., 21, and Jonathan Kandell, *La Capital: The Biography of Mexico City* (New York: Random House, 1988), 186-187.

7. Maza, *Catarina de San Juan: princesa de la India y visionaria de Puebla*, 21-22, and Frances Toor, *A Treasury of Mexican Folkways* (New York: Crown Publishers, 1947), 533.

8. Maza, *Catarina de San Juan: princesa de la India y visionaria de Puebla*, 43, 44, 47.

9. Ibid., 26-27.

10. Ibid., 37, 39.

11. Ibid., 40-41.

12. Ibid., 44; and Octavio Paz, *Sor Juana Or, The Traps of Faith* (Cambridge, Massachusetts: The Belknap Press of Harvard University Press, 1988), 122-123.

13. Maza, *Catarina de San Juan: princesa de la India y visionaria de Puebla*, 57-59; and Colin MacLachlan and Jaime E. Rodriguez O., *The Forging of the Cosmic Race: A Reinterpretation of Colonial Mexico* (Berkeley, Los Angeles, London: University of California Press, 1980), 234.

14. Maza, *Catarina de San Juan: princesa de la India y visionaria de Puebla*, 16.

15. Ibid., 61.

16. Ruth D. Lechuga, *El Traje Indígena de Mexico* (Mexico, D.F.: Panorama Editorial, S.A., 1986), 115-116.

17. Toor, *A Treasury of Mexican Folkways*, 288, 533.

18. Ibid., 533-535.

19. *Enciclopedia de México, Tomo II* (Ciudad de México, S.A.: El Instituto de la Enciclopedia de México, 1974), 215-216.

20. Maza, *Catarina de San Juan: princesa de la India y visionaria de Puebla*, 41, 52, 53, 61, 106-107.

21. Ibid., 15, 47, 108, 111, 114. Palafox, from Spain, came to Puebla as bishop in 1640. He quarreled bitterly with the Jesuits over their privileges, which he believed they abused. This led to his excommunicating those who attended Jesuit churches. Palafox returned to Spain in 1649, in fear for his life. *The Columbia Encyclopedia, Second Edition* (Morningside Heights, New York: Columbia University Press, 1950) 1471-1472.

Sor Juana Inés de la Cruz
The Tenth Muse

A certificate of baptism in the parish records of Chimalhuacán revealed that on December 2, 1648, an infant girl, Inés, was entered as a "daughter of the church." This euphemistic phrase indicated illegitimacy and was an inauspicious beginning for a child destined to be hailed as the greatest poet of colonial New Spain.

Juana Inés de Asbaje y Ramírez was born on November 12, 1648, in San Miguel Nepantla. Her godparents, Beatriz Ramírez and Miguel Ramírez, were the sister and brother of her mother. The church did not register the names of parents of children born out of wedlock.[1] Juana was the third illegitimate daughter of Isabel Ramírez de Santillana and Pedro Manuel de Asbaje y Vargas Machuca. Her mother was creole and her father, a military officer, came from the Basque provinces of Spain. Nothing else was learned about Asbaje, neither his temperament nor his influence. When he deserted his family, Isabel took another soldier into her home: Captain Diego Ruiz

Lozano, who fathered two more daughters and a son, also illegitimate.[2]

That Isabel Ramírez never married was not an unusual circumstance. She was a strong, independent woman, able to manage without the sanction of holy matrimony. In the seventeenth century, marriages were often arranged for social and economic reasons, particularly in the middle and upper classes. Isabel, a member of neither group, saw no advantage to legitimizing her unions because all children were accepted by families, no matter the situation of their birth.[3]

Juana Inés's own independent nature asserted itself from a very early age. In her *Reply to Sister Philothea*, written in 1691, she revealed that before her third birthday she followed an older sister to school and was filled with an overwhelming hunger to read. She believed she tricked the teacher by saying her mother also wished her to receive instruction. The kindly woman went along with the harmless ruse, and by the time her mother discovered her whereabouts, Juana was reading.[4]

She gave further evidence of her single-mindedness and passion for learning when she wrote in the *Reply* that she stopped eating cheese when, as a child, she heard "it made you stupid."[5]

By the age of five, Juana Inés's curiosity was greater than other children of a similar age. The spirited child asked questions and demanded answers adults were hard pressed to give. Knowledge of the printed word opened a world of endless possibilities for the child and, by six or seven, she read any page placed within her reach. Juana expressed her original thoughts in clever stories and understood both the significance and application of numbers. Then she began to write poetry and, before her eighth birthday, composed a *loa* to introduce a play for the Corpus Christi festival. She also learned to sew and embroider, a requisite for all young women.[6]

Sor Juana Inéz de la Cruz, the Tenth Muse

Portrait by Miguel Cabrera, 1750. Courtesy of the Nettie Lee Benson Latin American Collection, The General Libraries, The University of Texas at Austin.

Next, the family moved from the farmhouse in San Miguel Nepantla to the hacienda in Panoayán. Both of these were leased from the church by her maternal grandfather, Pedro Ramírez. Isabel assumed control of her father's hacienda after he died in January 1656 and remained in charge until she died in 1688. Then her daughter María took over up to her own death. It required great strength and resolve for these women to support themselves and their families, to supervise their laborers, and earn the respect of their neighbors.

Juana was about eight years old at this time. Several books, possibly acquired as furnishings, cluttered the desk and shelves in her grandfather's house. She read them all, committing to memory the assorted facts contained in these volumes of an indiscriminate nature. The amount of information that she, a child, acquired from this early study astonished the adults she would later meet in the capital.[7]

Juana heard of schools of higher learning in Mexico City. She begged her mother to allow her to cut her hair and dress as a man so she might attend classes. Permission was understandably denied. Her grandfather's books had kindled a passion for a formal education under the guidance of teachers. Her appetite for learning was insatiable. In her *Reply* she told of suffering "punishments and reproofs"[8] from her tenacious pursuit of the printed word. She did not indicate the reasons for this or who punished her. Perhaps Isabel realized the unlikeliness of a formal education and wanted to turn Juana's energies in a more practical direction, one suitable for women. Isabel was a sensible woman accustomed to the harshness of rural life. She understood the realities for one of Juana's background.

Sometime after the move and her grandfather's death, Juana went to Mexico City to live with her maternal aunt, Doña María Ramírez, and her wealthy husband, Juan de

Mata. The reasons for this move are obscure. Had life at the Panoayán hacienda become complicated by her mother's new lover and the birth of another illegitimate child? Were there financial reasons that influenced this decision and did her older sisters also leave? Surely Isabel recognized Juana's exceptional potential and considered the advantages of a city upbringing in her sister's home.[9]

Juana lived with the Matas for eight years but did not offer much information about this period in her writings. Undoubtedly the Matas provided her opportunities to study. In her *Reply* she revealed that in an attempt to learn Latin she set a timeframe for accomplishing certain tasks by cutting off "four or five finger widths" of her hair. If she did not achieve mastery by the time it grew back, she would cut it again as punishment for being a slow learner. Martín de Olivas came to the Matas house to teach Juana Latin, which she mastered in twenty lessons. Being able to read the great poets and classical writers broadened her horizons as she absorbed the literature and mythology of Greece and Rome. When she completed her studies in Latin, she began to study Portuguese, Italian, and Basque, the language of her father.[10]

Women in the seventeenth century were denied access to centers of higher learning. A young woman from a well-to-do family was prepared for life if she could read, embroider, and play a musical instrument. Some children of wealthy Spaniards and the descendants of Spaniards married to Mexican women attended schools, but most parents engaged teachers to come to their homes or hired tutors to live with them. Few Indian or mestizo children were fortunate enough to go to church schools.[11]

Meanwhile, news of the gifted girl spread throughout Mexico City reaching the ears of the new viceroy from Spain, Don Antonio Sebastián de Toledo, *marquis de Mancera*, and his wife, the *marquise* Doña Leonor Carreto. Juana's relatives requested permission to present their niece at court, and she was accepted as lady-in-waiting to the vicereine when she was fifteen years old.[12] Petitions for these positions at court came from wealthy parents who hoped their daughters might attract suitable husbands at the viceroy's palace. It was a duty of the court to help in the education and social refinement of many young people.[13] However, this petition from the family of a young person of questionable birth was unusual. Juana's beauty and intellect transcended any doubts about her parentage. Doña Leonor, an intelligent woman accustomed to making her own decisions, knew Juana would be a delightful and stimulating companion.

Juana thrived as a darling of the court. The palace was lively with receptions, balls, formal ceremonies, and flirtatious games. Many young men admired her considerable charms. The vicereine encouraged the continuation of her studies, and there was an audience appreciative of her intellect and talent as a poet. She created sensitive poems to celebrate birthdays and declare love or penned notes of sympathy in times of illness and death. She also wrote delightful witty rhymes, and her comedy plays were performed at the homes of the rich. Many poems of this period honored Doña Leonor. The depth of her feelings went far beyond her years. Words seemed to come without effort, and she remarked to friends at court that it was easier to write poetry than prose.[14]

The viceroy decided to have her intelligence publicly tested. He invited several distinguished professors from the university in Mexico City to the palace. About forty renowned scholars representing the arts, sciences, and assorted disciplines came to challenge her intelligence. There were theologians, poets, scripturists, philosophers, mathematicians, historians, and humanists. Though she had not prepared for this examination, Juana, poised, self-assured, and composed, amazed everyone with her brilliant responses.[15]

As her fame increased, so did the demands on her time and the infringement on her privacy. There was little time to devote to her books. Rumors circulated in the court of a secret romance, perhaps a broken heart. Some said she received many proposals of marriage. Considering her beauty and the romantic nature of her poetry, such speculation was not without merit. While members of the viceroy's court wondered among themselves, Juana herself never responded to their queries, and all that remained was romantic supposition.

Suddenly, she announced she wished to enter a convent. Juana, quite rightly, understood that a young woman had two choices: marriage or a convent. Typically marriages were arranged by families; love was of no concern. But Juana was a bastard without a name or a dowry. A dowry was expected at all economic levels in the seventeenth century. Relatives and neighbors contributed money or goods, if needed. Often a sizeable dowry made the difference for a woman hoping to rise above her social class. By law, the husband managed the dowry, but it belonged to the wife and absolute control remained with her.[16]

Marriage was not a valid option for Juana nor was managing a household to her taste. In her *Reply to Sister Philothea*, she explained that although she saw disadvantages for herself in becoming a nun, she preferred that way of life to one as a wife.[17]

Father Antonio Núñez de Miranda, confessor for the viceroy and vicereine, dedicated himself to acquainting young girls with the joys of becoming nuns. He obtained dowries for poor candidates who sought the protection of the convent and arranged to have Juana's dowry of three thousand pesos paid by her charitable sponsor, Captain Pedro Velázquez de la Cadena. Entrance into a convent was no different from contracting a marriage: each required a dowry. Núñez encouraged Juana to enter a convent believing it would result in a greater study of God, which he saw as her primary obligation. Núñez feared her popularity in the court would lure other young women to secular pursuits.[18]

Juana's decision to become a nun rested on many factors. The viceroy was due to be called back to Spain. He was already serving his second term and would leave Mexico in 1673. Furthermore, she was famous for a brilliant mind, and the church frowned upon her involvement in secular matters. Doña Leonor probably advised her to seek the refuge of a convent. A new viceroy might not be willing to act as her protector, and as a creole in a Spanish court, her position was not assured.[19]

Although Juana clearly stated her motives for choosing the convent, many looked for other reasons. There was no evidence to link her decision to romantic disappointment or to latent piety. Marriage, as she explained in her *Reply*, meant subjugation to a husband who would interfere with her studies. She had tired of the demands of court life and wished to live quietly, away from worldly distractions that took time away from her books and experiments. It was not prudent for a woman to live alone and she needed shelter and protection. The convent was the logical choice.

Social conditions in the seventeenth century fostered immorality. The politics of the viceroys conflicted with those of the church, and a caste system created by the cohabitation of several races brought on the evils of prejudice and discrimination. The reality of starvation forced women into prostitution, and even the upper classes flirted with misalliances. In an endeavor to keep women off the streets, the church offered protection by building convents and *recogimientos*, retreats. The clergy enticed young women with promises of shelter and then virtually imprisoned them.[20]

Shortly before her twentieth birthday, on August 14, 1667, Juana entered the convent of *San José de las Carmelitas Descalzas*, the Discalced (Barefoot) Carmelites. Why she chose this austere institution was unclear, perhaps she believed it would provide greater privacy for her studies. Nevertheless, the harsh conditions were not to her liking, and after three months she left. She did not retire to her own home or that of the Matas. She went instead to the palace, which had become her home. More than a year later she entered the convent of *San Jerónimo*. She took her vows on February 24, 1669, and became Sor Juana Inés de la Cruz (Sister Juana Inés of the Cross).

Upon her entrance to the order, it was necessary to say that she was the legitimate daughter of Pedro de Asbaje and Isabel Ramírez. Legitimacy, as well as the ability to pay assorted costs, was required for acceptance. Convent expenses included the purchase of clothing and a cell, providing for a servant or slave, and a yearly allowance. Father Núñez assumed the role of sponsor, along with Velázquez, to cover the expense of her dowry and ceremony of profession. His delight in snaring such a notable personage for the convent inspired him to invite many important representatives from the religious and secular community to celebrate the occasion.[21]

The term cell was misleading. At *San Jerónimo* nuns lived comfortably in private rooms, more like apartments. Each cell had enough room for guests and servants. A bill of sale shows Sor Juana had a two-story apartment with a sitting room, kitchen, bathroom, and bedrooms. Her mother sent her a mulatto slave when she took her vows. This slave, Juana de San José, was four years younger than Sor Juana and lived at the convent for ten years until she became pregnant. She was then sold, along with her infant son, to Sor Juana's sister Josefa, for two hundred and fifty gold pesos. In 1673 the cell was also home to two young nieces, daughters of her half-brother. Later another niece, Isabel María de San José, stayed until taking her own vows. It was a common practice to place young women under the care of nuns who saw to their educations.[22]

A nun at *San Jerónimo* wore a white full-sleeved tunic covered by a black scapular. The coif was white and the veil was black. An escutcheon bearing a religious scene hung over the scapular and a black thong representing the order of St. Augustine encircled the waist. A large rosary completed the habit.[23]

Juana realized before entering the convent that there would be certain communal obligation. If, however, she chose the convent to give her the freedom for solitary study, she was disappointed. Besides the responsibility of *contadora*, convent treasurer, plays and poems celebrating religious occasions needed composing. Noise from adjoining cells, music, conversations, and bickering between servants distracted her. There was no letup to the demands upon her time from the secular world. Visitors awaited her in the convent social rooms to exchange ideas or to request help. Often it was late at night before she returned to her books, experiments, and personal letters.[24]

Eventually the pursuit of her studies, at the expense of her religious devotions, and the secular leanings in her writing led to serious problems with Father Núñez. He demanded a cessation to this activity. The fact that her writing, censored by the Inquisition and not allowed publication in Mexico, was circulated in Spain caused ill will. There were other nuns who wrote convent histories, biographies, poems, and personal accounts of their lives, but none received the acclaim and attention of Sor Juana.[25]

Next a letter she wrote, but never intended to make public, was published. In it she analyzed the ideas used in a 1650 sermon by Antonio de Vieyra, a Portuguese Jesuit in Lisbon. In November 1690, a rebuke came from the bishop of Puebla, Don Manuel Fernández de Santa Cruz, who was responsible for the publication of this letter. Writing in cajoling terms, under the pseudonym Sor Filotea de la Cruz, the bishop cautioned against the sin of pride, suggesting her time would be better used studying the teachings of the church.[26]

Her response, *Repuesta a Sor Filotea de la Cruz* (Reply to Sister Philothea of the Cross), dated March 1, 1691, defended her right, and the rights of all women, to study both secular and theological matters. She said all women had the right to be educated, and they should not be forced to obey without question the orders of men. Sor Juana examined her life and work. She wrote about her compulsion to study all matter of God's creation and to question and learn. She revealed that when directly ordered to stop her studies for a period of three months, she was unable to turn her mind from observations of form, shape, even the mysteries of the egg. She offered anecdotes from her childhood in defense of herself as a nun with an unquenchable thirst for knowledge.[27]

Meanwhile, economic conditions in Mexico were worsening due to floods, famine, disease, and their aftermaths. People became violent, angered by excesses flaunted by the wealthy while the poor slaved for low wages and their children starved. In 1692 racial and social resentments in Mexico City triggered a devastating riot. Sor Juana's friends and protectors, preoccupied with their own destinies, no longer could be counted on for support.[28]

In 1693 Núñez reappeared as an influential person in her life. She agreed to confess the sin of her religious lapse and to embark upon a rededication to the church. Her confession lasted several weeks. It was signed in blood. At this time she relinquished her vast library of four thousand books, scientific materials, and musical instruments to the Archbishop of Mexico, Francisco Aguiar y Seijas. These were sold to raise money for the poor. The archbishop later confiscated other items of value. She kept only a few religious books, hair shirts, and items for self-mortification. In March of 1695 an unidentified epidemic devastated the city of Mexico. Sor Juana nursed the suffering nuns before falling ill herself. When she died on April 17, 1695, at the age of forty-six, she was buried in the same manner as other nuns at the convent.[29]

Sor Juana believed strongly in education for women and that they should be allowed to teach. It saddened her to see how lightly the accomplishments of women were treated. Her poetry expressed these feelings in an age when such sentiment was best left unspoken. She suffered criticism for defending the rights of women and for protesting their subordinate position. Many years passed before others found the courage to take up these causes.

Sor Juana Inés de la Cruz was called the "Nun of Mexico" and honored as the "Tenth Muse." According to ancient Greek mythology, there were nine muses who inspired creativity. The tenth muse, the guiding genius, is the great poet.

NOTES ON CHAPTER THREE

1. Octavio Paz, Margaret Sayre Peden, tr., *Sor Juana Or, The Traps of Faith* (Cambridge, Massachusetts: The Belknap Press of Harvard University Press, 1988), 1, 65. Paz says that scholars have changed the year of her birth, 1651, as was stated by the Jesuit priest Diego Calleja in his biography of Sor Juana.
2. Ibid., 65.
3. Colin M. MacLachlan and Jaime E. Rodriguez O., *The Forging of the Cosmic Race: A Reinterpretation of Colonial Mexico* (Berkeley, Los Angeles, London: University of California Press, 1980) 230-232, and Paz, *Sor Juana, Or The Traps of Faith*, 65-67.
4. Alan S. Trueblood, *tr., A Sor Juana Anthology* (Cambridge, Massachusetts, and London, England: Harvard University Press, 1988), 210-211.
5. Ibid., 211.
6. Carlos González Peña; Gusta Barfield Nance and Florene Johnson Dunstan, trs., *History of Mexican Literature: Third Edition* (Dallas: Southern Methodist Press, 1968), 111. A *loa* is a short commentary of praise offered as the prologue of a play.
7. Paz, *Sor Juana Or, The Traps of Faith*, 67, 86. Paz attributes the information about the books to Father Calleja.
8. Trueblood, tr., *A Sor Juana Anthology*, 211.
9. Paz, *Sor Juana Or, The Traps of Faith*, 86-87. Paz believes it was the death of Isabel's father's and the appearance of Diego Ruiz Lozano that caused Isabel to send Juana to the Matas.
10. Trueblood, tr., *A Sor Juana Anthology*, 211; and George H. Tavard, *Juana Inés de la Cruz and the Theology of Beauty: The First Mexican Theology* (Notre Dame, London: University of Notre Dame Press, 1991), 13-14.

11. Jonathan Kandell, *La Capital: The Biography of Mexico City* (New York: Random House, 1988), 213.

12. Paz, *Sor Juana Or, The Traps of Faith*, 88.

13. Tavard, *Juana Inés de la Cruz and the Theology of Beauty: The First Mexican Theology*, 3.

14. González Peña, *History of Mexican Literature: Third Edition*, 112, and Trueblood, tr., *A Sor Juana Anthology*, 4-5.

15. González Peña, *History of Mexican Literature: Third Edition*, 112, and Paz, *Sor Juana Or, The Traps of Faith*, 98.

16. MacLachlan and Rodriguez O., *The Forging of the Cosmic Race: A Reinterpretation of Colonial Mexico*, 242-243.

17. Trueblood, tr., *A Sor Juana Anthology*, 212.

18. Paz, *Sor Juana Or, The Traps of Faith*, 107-108; Stephanie Merrim, ed., *Feminist Perspectives on Sor Juana Inés de la Cruz* (Detroit: Wayne State University, 1991), Asunción Lavrin, "Unlike Sor Juana? The Model Nun in the Religious Literature of Colonial Mexico," 62; Kandell, *La Capital: The Biography of Mexico City*, 223.

19. Paz, *Sor Juana Or, The Traps of Faith*, 107-108, and Merrim, ed., *Feminist Perspectives on Sor Juana Inés de la Cruz*, Dorothy Schons, "Some Obscure Points in the Life of Sor Juana Inés de la Cruz," 38-40, 44-45.

20. Ibid., 40-41; and Kandell, *La Capital: The Biography of Mexico City*, 195-221. *Recogimiento* is a retreat or a house of correction for women.

21. Paz, *Sor Juana Or, The Traps of Faith*, 98, 99, 108, 109.

22. Ibid., 128; and Tavard, *Juana Inés de la Cruz and the Theology of Beauty: The First Mexican Theology*, 5.

23. Paz, *Sor Juana Or, The Traps of Faith*, 124.

24. Ibid., 127, 129; and Tavard, *Juana Inés de la Cruz and the Theology of Beauty: The First Mexican Theology*, 5.

25. Merrim, ed., *Feminist Perspectives on Sor Juana Inés de la Cruz*, Lavrin, "Unlike Sor Juana? The Model Nun in the Religious Literature of Colonial Mexico," 75, and Schons, "Some Obscure Points in the Life of Sor Juana Inés de la Cruz," 47, 49.

26. Paz, *Sor Juana Or, The Traps of Faith*, 395-397.

27. Trueblood, tr., *A Sor Juana Anthology*, "The Reply to Sor Philothea," 205-243.

28. Merrim, ed., *Feminist Perspectives on Sor Juana Inés de la Cruz*, Schons, "Some Obscure Points in the Life of Sor Juana Inés de la Cruz," 54-55, and Kandell, *La Capital: The Biography of Mexico City*, 230-231.

29. Paz, *Sor Juana Or, The Traps of Faith*, 459-464, 467; and Trueblood, tr., *A Sor Juana Anthology*, 10.

CHAPTER FOUR

María Josefa Ortiz
de Domínguez
La Corregidora

María Josefa Ortiz was born in Mexico City in 1773,[1] a time of great wealth and great poverty in the capital. Her father's position as a captain in the Spanish army enabled his creole family to enjoy a comfortable life, far removed from the barefoot peasants and the economic disasters of the city. Although the streets teemed with examples of destitution, it is unlikely that her family's life was greatly affected by the poor of the city.[2]

Josefa's father, José Ortiz Vázquez, a Spaniard born in 1714 in Mexico City, married three times and each time to women named Manuela. María Josefa was the daughter of his third marriage to Manuela Téllez Girón, a creole thirty-four years younger than her husband.[3]

Josefa's mother died when she was four years old, her father seven years later. The orphaned girl was left in the care of an older half-sister, María Sotero Ortiz. María used the small inheritance left by their father to send Josefa to school at the *colegio de las Vizcaínas*. She received a basic education in keeping with the general attitude of that age. There was a tacit agreement between school authorities and parents that it was unnecessary for young Mexican women to master the skill of writing. This was a joint endeavor to discourage amorous relations conducted through love letters, which, for a few pesos, were secreted over the convent walls.[4]

Students at *Vizcaínas* lived in small houses with three rooms and a kitchen. A house mother presided over each group of nine young women and supervised routine matters of dress, food, incidental expenses, and domestic chores. The oldest girl in the house, who may have been Josefa during her residency, was the leader. The young women studied reading, numbers, fine sewing and embroidery, music, and some writing. This curriculum was a matter of national policy, which governed these institutions and dictated the courses to be offered at most boarding schools.[5]

Josefa's experience at the school, living as a gently impoverished orphan, was demeaning. Perhaps her empathy for the poor Indians and mestizos under Spanish domination, whom she would later defend so courageously, began here. Even though she later came to enjoy a life of material comfort and social prestige, she identified with the downtrodden and was regarded as a friend and benefactor to those in need.[6]

Josefa was twelve years old in 1785 when she first entered the *colegio* as a boarding student. There is no explanation for her withdrawal after one year nor for her re-entrance three years later. The reason was probably financial, as the guarantor for her expenses differed each time. She was assigned the same registration number, 516, upon her return to school in 1789.[7]

Doña María Josefa Ortiz

Esposa de don Miguel Domínguez, corregidor de Querétaro. From México a través de los siglos. *Vicente Riva Palacia. Courtesy of the Nettie Lee Benson Latin American Collection, The General Libraries, The University of Texas at Austin.*

In the early months of 1791, María Sotero Ortiz informed the school that she was permanently withdrawing Josefa. Josefa was ill and no longer wished to remain at school, she wrote. However, the reason for this early departure was Josefa's relationship with Miguel Domínguez, a middle-aged widower with two daughters who was eager to begin a new life. When she left school, Josefa became pregnant with her first child. María Ignacia was born January 25, 1792. One year later, January 24, 1793, she married Miguel. Josefa gave birth to fourteen children, from 1792 through 1812; twelve survived. One died at birth and another at the age of two months.[8]

The beginning of the nineteenth century saw power in Mexico as an exclusive right of the *peninsulares*. These men, born in Spain, occupied the important government posts and the high positions in the Roman Catholic Church. Creoles, those born of Spanish parents in New Spain, held government or church positions of lesser importance and could own land in their own right. They contrasted greatly with the Indians and mestizos who worked long hours for little money and lived in abject poverty. Mestizos, offspring of mixed white and Indian unions, worked as farmers, laborers, or craftsmen and lived in small shacks bordering the cities. Some held better jobs as mine foremen or managers of haciendas. By government decree, mestizos lived apart from the Indians. The Indians, who were little better than slaves, were confined to ghetto-like conditions in their own villages and scratched a meager sustenance from communal fields allocated to them by the government. Although legally free men, the Indians were conscripted by government administrators whenever needed to build roads or buildings.[9]

Don Miguel had practiced law in Mexico City for five years when, in 1801, he was named *corregidor* of the town of Querétaro. This appointment brought him a salary of

four thousand pesos, in addition to income from unidentified sources. It was a reward for his diligent work for the
Spanish viceroy in the capital and an honor for a creole.
The government acknowledged Don Miguel as a man
who could be trusted in both public and private affairs.

He was sent to investigate and reform the abusive
conditions in the cloth factories of Querétaro. As chief
magistrate, it was his responsibility to see the Indians
obtained just treatment in business and government ne-
gotiations, but his commitment to protecting and bringing
relief to them was unusual. He successfully improved
workshop conditions for the Indians and mestizos and in
doing so earned their loyalty. However, the zeal with
which he executed his orders angered the European owners of the cloth mills.[10]

Don Miguel's reticent nature, his love of literature, and
his conservative politics contrasted with his wife's lively
and outspoken nature. Doña Josefa managed the household, cared for her growing family, prepared for frequent
guests, and left official policies to him. Their home in
Querétaro was on the second floor of the *Palacio Municipal*.
It was common for appointed officials to live in rooms
above government offices used for commerce and occupied by public servants.

Their personal rooms upstairs, reached through a private door, became a gathering place for important people
passing through the town.[11] Doctors, lawyers, teachers,
and army officers alike sat in finely carved chairs from
Spain and sipped chocolate from fragile china cups
while Doña Josefa, dressed in a dark silk dress, her hair
braided fashionably at her neck, presided as hostess in her
drawing room.

Although removed from the politics in Mexico City,
they often discussed the disquieting news from the capital. Prominent creoles believed it was time to take over the
government of Mexico. However, the Spaniards were

prepared to stay even if that meant imprisoning the agita-
tors. The creoles, amassing resentments against the
Spanish *gachupines*, met in small secret groups to discuss
their grievances. (*Gachupines* was a derisive term for the
Spaniards that was literally translated as wearer of spurs.
It was first used to describe the Spanish conquerors and
early settlers of New Spain.[12]) Inspired by what they read
about the American and French Revolutions, they discussed liberty and equality as it pertained to their own
situation. Their agenda focused on ridding the country of
Spanish domination, abolishing slavery, improving living
conditions for the poor, and educating all children, including Indian. In essence, it was equal rights for all Mexico's
people.[13]

The most important group was organized by Don
Ignacio Allende, a captain in the Queen's Cavalry Regiment in Guanajuato. It met regularly at the *corregidor's*
house in Querétaro under the guise of a "literary society."
Allende introduced Doña Josefa to the ideas of Father
Miguel Hidalgo and rallied the group of conspirators. The
captain had befriended Hidalgo a few years after the
cleric's arrival in Dolores and brought him into contact
with a select group of friends.

The handsome Allende, a well-to-do landowner, had
bristled when a Spanish official referred to his creole
inferiority, and he was determined to bring an end to
Spanish domination. He had a reputation for daring as a
horseman and in the bullring. During a feat of bravado, he
sustained a crippling injury to his left arm, but he felt
inferior to no man. Allende stood out as a leading advo-
cate for independence, dedicating himself to the cause of
the downtrodden and defenseless populace.[14] A close
relationship developed between Doña Josefa and the
young man. This supposedly was based on his engage-
ment to one of her daughters; however, there are
indications he was already married.[15]

Doña Josefa welcomed him in her home, for whatever reason, and he encouraged her participation in the
conspiracy. This was not the first indication of the *corregidora's* interest in freedom from Spanish domination. José
Joaquín Fernández de Lizardi, an author and editor of a
weekly newspaper, often visited Don Miguel and Doña
Josefa in their home in Mexico City to discuss independence for Mexico.[16]

The Querétaro group was comprised of well-to-do
creoles, military officers, and priests. It met in the drawing
room of the *corregidora's* home under the pretense of
discussing literature, but the only literary materials were
the pamphlets written by Hidalgo and the discussions
focused on means to overcome the royalist political
machine. It appears Hidalgo did not often attend these
meetings at Doña Josefa's home, but met with the revolutionists at other locations to discuss independence.[17]

Miguel Hidalgo y Costilla was also a creole. His father,
the manager of a large hacienda, had sent Miguel and
his older brother, José Joaquín, to the Jesuit college in
Valladolid. When the Spanish King Charles III banished
the Jesuits from the Spanish possessions in the New
World, including New Spain, the boys were left without
teachers and sent home. Less than a year later, they
returned to Valladolid to the *colegio de San Nicolás Obispo.*
Hidalgo studied Latin, theology, and rhetoric, and continued learning the Indian languages he heard as a boy on
the hacienda. He became a priest in 1778 and returned to
San Nicolás as a teacher.

Father Hidalgo was notorious for gambling, dancing,
reading books condemned by the church, and his romantic liaisons, which flaunted the vow of celibacy. When he
moved to the small parish of Dolores in 1803 at the age of
fifty, he brought along members of his family, including
two illegitimate daughters. Hidalgo delegated his religious duties to a parish vicar, then he challenged himself to

improve the lives and economy of his Indian parishioners. He set up small workshops for pottery making, tanning, carpentry, wool weaving, beekeeping, silk growing, harness making, and blacksmithing. His attempts to produce wine and olive oil ran afoul of the government. Under the cover of producing goods, Hidalgo's small force was also making bullets and printing the pamphlets he wrote. His home was open to all castes; poor Indians mingled with wealthy townspeople to discuss current topics and literature and to dance, drink, and play lively parlor games.[18]

Doña Josefa was a practical woman, known to have a mind of her own, and she embraced the cause of independence wholeheartedly. Her gentle manners masked a determined spirit; the love she had previously lavished only on her family she now focused on her country. Don Miguel initially opposed the conspiracy, but his wife's passionate enthusiasm for the cause convinced him to join her in secretly supporting the revolutionists. His position as *corregidor* exposed him daily to injustices suffered by the Indians, mestizos, and black slaves. When he spoke of these conditions to his wife, it was only in the privacy of their bedroom. It would be dangerous to mention certain things in front of the wrong people. Other visitors openly discussed government affairs in their home. As wife of the *corregidor*, Doña Josefa was above suspicion. She sat, quietly embroidering, between visiting Spanish officers and listened to their plans. At times, she overheard useful information, which she passed on to the insurgents, thus becoming an important link for the leaders of the revolution.

There are questions about her literacy and ability to write. Records from her school refer to this, yet copies of some of her letters exist. There is no doubt that she could read even if she lacked proficiency in penmanship. When it became necessary for her to send a message, she cut words from various documents at her disposal and pasted them on sheets of paper. This served two purposes: it assured that her co-conspirators could read her messages and protected her identity.[19]

During the summer of 1810, information about the plot to overthrow the Spanish reached the government in the capital by way of Mariano Galván, a post office clerk who acted as secretary at the secret meetings in Querétaro. This news was not unexpected as the denouncement of an earlier uprising, the Valladolid Conspiracy, had alerted the capital to creole unrest. Hidalgo knew about that aborted revolt but was not officially connected with it. The information about the Querétaro involvement led the authorities to order the arrest of Allende, Hidalgo, and Juan de Aldama, another conspirator, but Allende intercepted the order.[20]

Then on the tenth of September, a more serious accusation came from Joaquín Arias, captain of the company at Celaya and a conspirator. Arias was afraid the conspiracy had been discovered and was anxious to absolve himself of complicity. Using this information, Juan de Ochoa, the mayor of Querétaro, ordered his *escribiano*, Juan Fernando Domínguez, to prepare a statement for the viceroy implicating the *corregidor* and Doña Josefa. He further accused the *corregidora* of making loud and seditious statements against Spain and several of its ministers. He said that she had fomented dissatisfaction shamelessly among those attending her gatherings. Others, too, may have approached the authorities with news of the plot to protect themselves.[21]

Don Miguel received orders to conduct a formal investigation and to place a watch on the garrison where the guns where kept. Pretending to be on the royalist side gave him additional time to alert Hidalgo and his followers. Then he approached the *escribiano* hoping to learn the source of the denouncement. On September 13, Don Miguel heard from a trusted friend that it would be prudent to initiate some action against those implicated in the plot in order to protect himself from imprisonment. It was possible that Doña Josefa overheard this message, which was delivered outside of their house. Don Miguel deployed a small force to surround the house of the brothers Emeterio and Epigmenio González and discovered a quantity of guns and ammunition. Perhaps, if the *corregidor* had not gone to see the *escribiano*, this search could have been avoided. Don Miguel earlier misdirected the search for arms; now he had no choice but to arrest the brothers.[22]

The *corregidor* feared Doña Josefa might act rashly and that her involvement in the plot would place her in danger. He ordered her to stay in the house and cautioned her against speaking to anyone who might betray them. Before he left, Don Miguel locked the entrance gates to their house. Doña Josefa knew the revelation of the plot not only endangered the lives of all the conspirators, but that the very success of the movement had been jeopardized. It was imperative to alert the leaders. She was prepared for this emergency and using a prearranged signal alerted the trusted jailer whose room was directly below hers. Ignacio Pérez, the warden of the prison, heard her foot tap three times on the floor of her bedroom. He came immediately to speak with her through the wicket grating of the locked room. She urged him to go at once to warn Captain Allende and Hidalgo of the betrayal.[23]

At the same time Don Miguel was searching for the cache of arms, Ignacio Pérez was on his way to San Miguel el Grande. Aldama was the first to receive the message and the two men raced to Dolores where Allende and Hidalgo were meeting. Meanwhile, at dawn on September 14, Doña Josefa sent her stepdaughter, accompanied by a priest, to alert Arias. She was unaware that Arias, camped in the town of Celaya supposedly awaiting a sign for the revolution to begin, had betrayed the conspirators in Querétaro. Ochoa planned to arrest Arias on the night of September 15. Incriminating letters planted in the officer's possession would force him to implicate the conspirators.[24]

The uprising was originally to begin December 8, 1810, during the annual fair at San Juan de los Lagos. This would coincide with the celebration of the miracle attributed to the *Virgen de Candelaria*. The leaders anticipated a gathering of at least 35,000 people, most of whom would be Indian and mestizo. They hoped to take advantage of their religious fervor to incite the crowd to topple the *gachupines* merchants at the fair and initiate the revolution. However, the plan was moved up to October 2 when Hidalgo determined a state of preparedness had been reached. Two hours past midnight on September 16, 1810, Aldama reached Dolores with the news of the betrayal. After speaking with Allende, the two men delivered Doña Josefa's news to Hidalgo who declared it was time to begin the revolution.[25]

At four o'clock in the morning of September 16, Don Miguel and Doña Josefa awakened to the noise of Spanish soldiers pounding on their door. They were placed under arrest and ordered to dress quickly. Fifteen others accused of conspiracy were arrested also. Ochoa escorted the *corregidor* to the convent of San Francisco, but when there was a delay in opening the gates, he was taken to the convent of Santa Cruz, placed in a cell, and kept in seclusion. Doña Josefa, although pregnant with her thirteenth child, went first to Ochoa's home and then to the convent in Santa Clara. She was forbidden to see her children or friends. Her daughters were not allowed to communicate with the servants who attended her. Don Miguel refused to give any information and managed to get a message to his wife advising her to maintain silence.[26]

A few hours later, in the early morning light, Father Miguel Hidalgo climbed the uneven stone steps in front of his small church in Dolores. He paused to look around the town square. It was a typical market day, the plaza alive with Indians and mestizos who had been arriving since dawn. The urgent ringing of the bells summoned them to the church. Standing in front of his people, Father Hidalgo called out to them to end tyranny and join him in the fight for independence. His outcry, the historic *grito* for freedom and justice for the average person, marked the start of the revolution.[27]

Juan Collado headed a commission sent by the viceroy to prosecute the conspirators. He released the *corregidor* from prison soon after his arrival in Querétaro. Collado considered it wise to free Don Miguel who was popular with the local Indians. Now that the revolution was in progress, he wanted to ward off reprisals, which could put him at risk. It was his official decision to drop all charges and reinstate the *corregidor*. Collado, anxious to leave the volatile situation in Querétaro, began the return trip to Mexico City, but on his way was captured by the rebels. The freedom of the conspirators from Querétaro, except for the Gonzalez brothers, was a condition of Collado's release. Doña Josefa was permitted later to return to her home due to special circumstances, meaning, no doubt, her pregnancy.[28]

Three years passed quietly. Don Miguel resumed his duties as chief magistrate; his wife again presided over the household. Then suddenly the viceroy, General Felix Calleja, ordered the arrest of Doña Josefa for her part in the revolution. This was after the birth of her fourteenth child. The viceroy was informed, by a confidential report, that an agent in Querétaro was speaking out against the legitimate Spanish government. The report by Archdeacon José Mariano Beristáin named the *corregidor's* wife and accused her of behaving like an "Ana Bolena."[29] In various documents, she was denounced as "notoriously scandalous, seductive, and destructive" and "impudent, bold and incorrigible."[30]

Viceroy Felix Calleja's initial reaction was to remove Don Miguel from office. Instead he issued an indictment, dated December 28, 1813, against Doña Josefa. On January 11, 1814, the *corregidor* personally surrendered his wife.[31]

The trip to Mexico City took two and a half days. She was allowed to take one servant. During the trip Doña Josefa harangued the royalist guards, insulting them, calling them cowards for not supporting Mexican independence. When a guard ordered her to be silent, she said it was his job to escort her to Mexico City, not to give her orders and she continued to speak her mind. When the soldiers offered her food, she refused it, eating only what she brought with her or could buy.[32]

She was taken to the convent of Santa Teresa and separated from the daughter who accompanied her on the trip. Don Miguel wrote to the viceroy pleading for her release, citing the tears of her twelve young children who witnessed her arrest, the youngest only eighteen months old. He begged for compassion acknowledging the dishonor to his family by accusations of sedition and other crimes of unknown origin.

Don Miguel resigned as *corregidor* and requested permission to appear in the capital to defend his wife. He wrote in detail of his more than twenty years of loyal service to the government and said that now, when he was nearly blind and in poor health, he was deprived of his wife. Don Miguel waited a month for a reply and then wrote again. Almost a month later, he was directed to leave his office in order and given permission to travel to the capital.[33]

Doña Josefa also wrote the viceroy from her prison for an audience. She complained about the absence of formal charges and of the indignities she suffered during the trip to the city. In a second letter she told of the bitterness of separation from her children and her husband and again requested an audience and an official statement of charges.[34]

Persecution continued even after her confinement, and her continued support of the rebel forces led to questions about her sanity. She was moved to the convent of Santa Catalina, sentenced to spend the next four years there. However, prison walls did not stop her support of independence. In 1816 viceroy Calleja returned to Spain. Don Miguel petitioned the new viceroy for her release, and on June 17, 1817, Doña Josefa was freed. She returned home to find their property had been confiscated by the government. It was never returned. Later she refused all offers of compensation for her contribution to the cause of freedom.[35]

Then Agustín de Iturbide and Vicente Guerrero joined forces to make Mexico independent. Iturbide proposed a plan to guarantee independence calling for a limited monarchy under an emperor, religious freedom, and unification of ideologies between Mexicans and Europeans. Official approval of The Plan of Iguala came on March 1, 1821, but the plan was not universally accepted. A rumor circulated that Doña Josefa had participated in its formation. This she vehemently disclaimed as slander and called both Guerrero, whom she had earlier supported, and Iturbide traitors.

She believed Guerrero compromised the issue of independence by accepting a political and not a social resolution. She said Iturbide, representing clergy and landowners, had disregarded the issues of the poor and castes. When Iturbide became emperor in 1822, he thought to honor Doña Josefa with the position of lady-in-waiting to his wife. She refused, saying her vision of an independent Mexico was not that of an empire.[36]

Doña Josefa never wavered in her fight for freedom and human rights. She spoke out against President

Guadalupe Victoria when he expelled the Spanish from Mexico, saying Mexico must be a country for all people. Her single-mindedness eventually caused a rift with her family over the policies of Vicente Guerrero.

In 1824 she chose to live apart from Don Miguel. She took only a servant with her. The years of imprisonment and persecution had taken their toll. Doña Josefa was frail and in poor health. She assembled her family to make her farewells shortly before her death in 1829. Burial took place at the convent of Santa Catalina, which was once her prison. Later the government returned her body with honors to Querétaro.[37]

The Mexican government declared her to be *"Benemérita de la Patria,"* great citizen of the country. The people of Mexico remember her as a great citizen of the world.

NOTES ON CHAPTER FOUR

1. José María Miquel i Vergés, *Diccionario de insurgentes* (Mexico: Editorial Porrúa, 1969), 440; and Gabriel Agraz García de Alba, *Los Corregidores Don Miguel Domínguez y Doña María Josefa Ortiz y el inicio de la independencia, Tomo I* (Mexico, D.F.: Edición del Autor, 1992), 1. Sources do not agree about the year and city of her birth: Valladolid (Morelia), 1768, or Mexico City, 1773.

2. Jonathan Kandell, *La Capital: The Biography of Mexico City* (New York: Random House, 1988), 254-255.

3. Agraz García de Alba, *Los Corregidores Don Miguel Domínguez y Doña María Josefa Ortiz y el inicio de la independencia, Tomo I*, 19.

4. Ibid., 27-28.

5. Ibid., 35.

6. Martha Cotera, *Profile on the Mexican American Woman* (Austin, Texas: National Educational Library Publishers, Inc., 1976), 37.

7. Agraz García de Alba, *Los Corregidores Don Miguel Domínguez y Doña María Josefa Ortiz y el inicio de la independencia, Tomo I*, 31-32.

8. Ibid., 35, 36, 39, 40.

9. Bob and Jan Young, *Liberators of Latin America*, (New York: Lothrop, Lee & Shepard Co., 1970), 145-147, and *The World Book Encyclopedia, Volume 13* (Chicago, London, Paris, Sydney, Tokyo, Toronto: World Book-Childcraft International, Inc., 1980), 384.

10. Ernest Gruening, *Mexico and Its Heritage* (New York: Appleton-Century-Crofts, Inc., 1928), 30, and Hugh M. Hamill, Jr., *The Hidalgo Revolt: Prelude to Mexican Independence* (Gainesville: University of Florida Press, 1966), 106; and Hubert Howe Bancroft, *History of*

Mexico, Volume XII, Vol. IV, 1804-1824 (San Francisco: The History Company, Publishers, 1886), footnote 114.

11. Verónica Zárate, colaboración, *Josefa Ortiz de Domínguez: La Corregidora*, Serie de Cuadernos Conmemorativos, Comisión Nacional para las Celebraciones del 175 Aniversario de la Independencia Nacional y 75 Aniversario de la Revolución Mexicana (Mexico: Instituto Nacional de Estudios Históricos de la Revolución Mexicana, Col. Juárez, C.P., 1985), 28; and Miquel i Vergés, *Diccionario de insurgentes*, 440.

12. James A. Magner, *Men of Mexico* (Freeport, New York: Books for Libraries Press, 1968), 151.

13. Elsa Larralde, *The Land and People of Mexico* (Philadelphia and New York: J.B. Lippincott Company, 1964), 66-67; and T.R. Fehrenbach, *Fire and Blood: A History of Mexico* (New York: Macmillan Publishing Co., Inc., 1973), 315; and Michael C. Meyer and William L. Sherman, *The Course of Mexican History: Third Edition* (New York, Oxford: Oxford University Press, 1987), 286.

14. Bancroft, *History of Mexico, Volume XII, Vol. IV, 1804-1824*, 104-105.

15. Ibid., 106; and Zárate, col., *Josefa Ortiz de Domínguez: La Corregidora*, 19.

16. Alfonso Teja Zabre, *Guide to the History of Mexico: A Modern Interpretation* (Austin, New York: The Pemberton Press, Jenkins Publishing Company, 1969), 267.

17. Zárate, col., *Josefa Ortiz de Domínguez: La Corregidora*, 19-20; and Bancroft, *History of Mexico, Volume XII, Vol. IV, 1804-1824*, 104.

18. Meyer and Sherman, *The Course of Mexican History: Third Edition*, 285-286, and Hamill, Jr., *The Hidalgo Revolt: Prelude to Mexican Independence*, 80-88.

19. Zárate, col., *Josefa Ortiz de Domínguez: La Corregidora*, 20-21; and *Enciclopedia de México, Tomo X* (Ciudad de

México, S.A.: Instituto de la Enciclopedia de México, 1974), 13.

20. Zárate, col., *Josefa Ortiz de Domínguez: La Corregidora*, 23; and Bancroft, *History of Mexico, Volume XII, Vol. IV, 1804-1824*, 110; and Hamill, Jr., *The Hidalgo Revolt*, 97, 101.

21. Zárate, col., *Josefa Ortiz de Domínguez: La Corregidora*, 23-24; and Hamill, Jr., *The Hidalgo Revolt*, 117.

22. Ibid., 27; and Bancroft, *History of Mexico, Volume XII, Vol. IV, 1804-1824*, 111-112.

23. Ibid., 112; and Zárate, col., *Josefa Ortiz de Domínguez: La Corregidora*, 28-29; and Agraz García de Alba, *Los Corregidores Don Miguel Domínguez y Doña María Josefa Ortiz y el inicio de la independencia*, 89.

24. Miquel i Vergés, *Diccionario de insurgentes*, 440.

25. Hamill, Jr., *The Hidalgo Revolt*, 113-114, 116; and Zárate, col., *Josefa Ortiz de Domínguez: La Corregidora*, 28.

26. Bancroft, *History of Mexico, Volume XII, Vol. IV, 1804-1824*, 113-114; and Agraz García de Alba, *Los Corregidores Don Miguel Domínguez y Doña María Josefa Ortiz y el inicio de la independencia*, 40, unpaged.

27. Meyer and Sherman, *The Course of Mexican History: Third Edition*, 287-288.

28. Bancroft, *History of Mexico, Volume XII, Vol. IV, 1804-1824*, 114, footnote 114-115; and Zárate, col., *Josefa Ortiz de Domínguez: La Corregidora*, 31.

29. Ibid., 31-32.

30. Agraz García de Alba, *Los Corregidores Don Miguel Domínguez y Doña María Josefa Ortiz y el inicio de la independencia*, 104.

31. Ibid., 107.

32. Ibid., 107-108.

33. Ibid., 108.

34. Ibid., 109.

35. Zárate, col., *Josefa Ortiz de Domínguez: La Corregidora,* 32; and Cotera, *Profile on the Mexican American Woman,* 38.

36. Irene Nicholson, *The Liberators: A Study of Independence Movements in Spanish America* (New York, Washington: Frederick A. Praeger, Publishers, 1969), 253.

37. Zárate, col., *Josefa Ortiz de Domínguez: La Corregidora,* 32; and Cotera, *Profile on the Mexican American Woman,* 38; and Agraz García de Alba, *Los Corregidores Don Miguel Domínguez y Doña María Josefa Ortiz y el inicio de la independencia,* 121-122.

Leona Vicario
Freedom Fighter

When Don Agustín Pomposo Fernández de San Salvador y Montiel learned of his sister's death in 1806, he immediately took upon himself the guardianship of his eighteen-year-old niece. The girl's father had died earlier that same year, and seeing to her well-being was a matter of his family responsibility as her godfather and uncle.

María de la Soledad Leona Camila Vicario Fernández de San Salvador was born in Mexico City on April 10, 1789. Her father, Gaspar Martín Vicario, was Spanish and a successful businessman who left a considerable fortune to his daughter. Her mother, Camila Fernández de San Salvador y Montiel, was a creole from a prominent family in Toluca.[1]

Leona, a product of such a fine background, was attractive, charming, and gracious. Thus, it pleased her uncle to be able to make living arrangements for his orphaned niece at *la número 19 de la calle de Don Juan Manuel* in Mexico City. Leona favored this house over others he considered and it was large enough to convert into two: one for her and a separate one for his own family. Here it would be convenient to attend to her best interests and still allow her to enjoy as much freedom as possible for a young woman in that era.

Furthermore, Don Agustín resolved to scrupulously manage her sizeable inheritance. No doubt Leona, accustomed to a life of comfort and already attended by several servants, was less frugal than her uncle deemed prudent. Controlling her expenses was a way to prevent her from squandering her patrimony. Leona, distracted by the recent loss of her parents, was equally pleased to have her uncle take over the details of finding such a house and managing her affairs. Don Agustín also insisted on paying one-half of his sister's funeral expenses and some of Leona's rent.

Leona moved into the new house accompanied by her former servants to begin its renovation and improvement. Her first directive was to change the wine cellar into a garage for her two carriages. When Doña Camila was in the final stages of her highly contagious disease, she had ordered her daughter to leave all her furnishings behind to prevent contamination. Leona, like her mother, had excellent taste and enjoyed the task of furnishing her new home. She selected a sofa with silk pillows, a desk, chairs, large tables, and cabinets to hold her fine china, silver, and goblets of golden crystal. She bought blue crystal candelabrum with golden accents, ornate mirrors, good paintings, and wash bowls made of balsam. Her personal items, a rosary of gold and pearls, silver brush and tortoiseshell comb, linens of fine chambray and lace, all reflected an innate appreciation of quality and good breeding.[2]

Don Agustín, meticulously surveying Leona's accounts, soon discovered the young woman spent money foolishly, as had her mother. There were costly improvements to the house and her personal upkeep and wages

Leona Vicario

From Leona Vicario, heroina insurgente *por Genaro García. Courtesy of the Nettie Lee Benson Latin American Collection, The General Libraries, The University of Texas at Austin.*

for the servants. Fortunately there were no jeweler's bills. Leona inherited exquisite jewelry from her mother: a collar containing fifty-one pearls, pear-shaped earrings set with diamonds, two eardrops of diamonds, and diamond chains. However, in his desire to act as her father, he denied her nothing, and it was not surprising that she went through thousands of dollars within the first months of her mother's death.[3]

In the early nineteenth century, the role of well-to-do creole women was clearly defined. The younger women idled away their days obsessed with their grooming, dressing in the latest fashions, and shopping. Lunch and a siesta completed the afternoon, and in the evenings there might be the theater to attend or perhaps a ball, always chaperoned by a *dueña*. Most of the women in New Spain were uneducated, but young women from better families learned to read, write, sew, and embroider and received religious instruction. Music or painting lessons were available for a talented few. A scholarly education was considered unnecessary as after their marriages they devoted themselves to household activities and their families.[4]

Leona was the exception. She was fortunate to have come from a family who believed in educating their daughter and placed her in the hands of excellent tutors. Leona studied history, science, languages, art, music, and literature. The knowledge of French introduced her to the writings of famous liberal French authors. Her formative years coincided with the time of the French Revolution, and she absorbed the ideas of independence proposed by these writers. While such works were banned in New Spain, these books circulated secretly and were fairly easy to obtain. Leona developed an interest in more serious matters, particularly politics. This was unusual and annoyed her uncle, a royalist supporter.[5]

Don Agustín, a rich and influential attorney in the capital, claimed a mixed heritage from native chieftains and European nobility. As lawyer for the *Real Audiencia* and the *Illustre Colegio*, he was an important official in the viceroyalty and was appointed a rector of the university three times.[6]

By arrangement with the law school, Andrés Quintana Roo, a recent graduate from the University of Mexico, worked as a legal assistant in the attorney's office. This experience was necessary before obtaining a license to practice law. He was born on November 30, 1787, in Mérida, the capital of Yucatán, and initially attended the theological seminary near his home. He then moved to Mexico City where he earned a bachelor's degree in liberal arts and canon law. It was at the home of Don Agustín that Leona met and fell in love with Andrés, a handsome, well-dressed young man with the soul of a poet.[7]

Leona was a pretty young woman with a pale pink complexion. She had a small mouth, round face, wide forehead, strong chin, and a perfect nose. She was of average height and had a striking figure. Andrés was charmed by her easy conversation and independent thinking. At an early age Leona earned a reputation for a rebellious streak and was not afraid to speak her mind. As a child she had heard about the noble blood, blue blood, running through her family's veins. When she noticed the blood of a relative was the same color as that of a servant who received a cut in an accident, she declared the only blue was that of the sky where every noble deed ascends, like those of her mother when she aided the poor.[8]

Leona and Andrés liked each other from their first encounter. They shared a passion for literature and political issues, particularly the cause of independence. After a proper interval, Andrés petitioned her uncle for Leona's hand in marriage. Don Agustín opposed the union. He explained that in keeping with the customs of the day she had been promised to a wealthy young man from a noble family in León, and he refused to nullify this contract. Leona was engaged to Octaviano de Obregón y Gómez, but the young man fled the country after his father got into trouble with the authorities.[9] However, a more probable reason for her uncle's refusal was the young man's revolutionary ideas.[10]

Don Agustín's son Manuel had recently joined the supporters of independence, and he was not about to lose the niece he thought of as a daughter to the same cause. Don Agustín was a realist and an ardent supporter of the royalists. Although he published some poetry, he turned to prose once the revolution began and was the author of several papers denouncing the insurgents who called themselves *guadalupes*. The insurgents had adopted the image of the Virgin of Guadalupe as their banner; this figure, called *la primera mestiza*, represented the essence of their cause. Their motto was: *"Viva nuestra madre santísima de Guadalupe, viva Fernando VII, viva la América y muera el mal gobierno."* (Long life to our most holy Mother of Guadalupe, long life to Fernando VII, long life to America and death to bad government.)[11]

In 1812 Quintana Roo abandoned his position in the lawyer's office to join the rebels in Michoacán who operated under the orders of Ignacio López Rayón. Rayón appealed to the intellectuals in Mexico City and ran an insurgent printing press. As a poet, Quintana Roo was ideally suited to writing articles advocating freedom and equality.[12] Don Agustín hoped the young man's absence would bring the girl to her senses. However, he had not considered the depth of her feeling for the young man. This, coupled with her romantic idealism of war, brought on a fanatical enthusiasm for the cause.

Many women, insurgent and royalist, took an active role in the independence movement. After the subservient roles played by women during the colonial period, they welcomed the opportunity to free themselves from the bonds of submission. While some supported the opinions of their families, there were others who openly or secretly defied these.

News of Doña Josefa's courageous actions in Querétaro and her continuing support of the cause from prison undoubtedly influenced some women, and Leona Vicario may have been one of those. Women from all social levels, countesses and nuns, housewives and greengrocers, were known to be spies and to fight, even die, at the side of their men. Others filled important positions as nurses, conspirators, strategists, and couriers.[13]

The War of Independence lasted for almost eleven years. The first stage, from 1810 to 1815, was called the popular rebellion. Its three main goals were: the establishment of a republic guaranteeing equality for all races, ending the special privileges enjoyed by the Roman Catholic Church and the army, and breaking up the large estates to make small farms for the people. The insurgents wanted representation in the government and were critical of the politics of Spain which affected their lives and caused economic hardship. Slowly, under the leadership of Hidalgo, Allende, Aldama, and others, the movement gathered momentum and people became more vocal in expressing their discontent.[14]

Although unable to leave home, Leona resolved to make a contribution to the cause and in 1812 began to participate in the movement. She corresponded with the *insurgentes* using the pseudonym Henriqueta.[15] As Pompaso's niece she was privy to information shared by royalist visitors in her uncle's drawing room and, like Doña Josefa, passed this on to the insurgents hiding in the mountains. She also relayed their messages to the conspirators in Mexico City. Her uncle was convinced that the separation from Quintana Roo had separated her from the independence movement. Far from it, Leona even recruited men from upper-class creole families to join their ranks. This possibly included her cousin, Pompaso's son. Leona devised a system to get money and supplies to the rebels through an underground railroad. She sold her jewels and used her inheritance to buy weapons. All this was accomplished under the very nose of her uncle, but even protected by family position, her activities eventually brought her under scrutiny by the authorities.[16]

Unexpectedly, Mariano Salazar, a muleteer, was exposed as her agent and some of her letters written in code[17] were intercepted. Don Agustín was furious and ordered her locked in the house. Leona, having already demonstrated her resourcefulness, escaped to the town of San Juanico in Tacuba. From there, she found shelter in San Joaquín with other women sympathetic to the cause. They urged her to return to her home, but she was determined to join Quintana Roo and the insurgents camped in Tlalpujahua. While hiding in San Joaquín at the home of her old governess, she was betrayed and apprehended by royalist soldiers who escorted her back to her uncle in Mexico City.[18]

Agustín Pompaso was a very influential man, a respected friend of the royalist government. His niece was an embarrassment. Nevertheless, he went before the viceroy on her behalf and managed to save her from imprisonment in the disreputable common jails. Instead she was confined in *el convento de Belén de las Mochas* and placed under the jurisdiction of the *Real Junta de Seguridad y Buen Orden*. The military commissioner assigned to her case tried various ways to force her to cooperate. When flattery failed, he tried terror and threatened to have her executed as a traitor. Finally after one lengthy interrogation, she was offered a life sentence in lieu of death if she would name her co-conspirators. Leona steadfastly answered their questions only as they applied to herself and refused to involve anyone else. She was returned to her cell.[19]

Fortunately, the convent was ill-prepared for an assault by the insurgent colonels: Francisco Arroyave, Antonio Vázquez Aldama, and Luis Rodríguez Alconedo. Late at night, on April 22, 1813, these three men, dressed in black, rode to the convent on horseback to rescue Leona. They broke through the locked gates and while two entered the convent to free her from her locked cell, the third waited outside to warn of approaching guards. Leona was carried away on an extra horse. As soon as possible, she was smuggled out of the city, hidden on a mule train which carried printer's type and paper for the insurgent press packed as fruit in crates. In pigskins, commonly used to transport *pulque*, a fermented juice, was ink. Leona, disguised in blackface and rags, was safe and on her way to Oaxaca to join the insurgents under the leadership of José María Morelos y Pavon.[20]

Morelos, a creole, was formerly a poor parish priest. When ordered by the bishop to post bans announcing the excommunication of Father Miguel Hidalgo, he refused and went to join Hidalgo as a chaplain in his army. Hidalgo had enough clerics and requested that Morelos return to his home to raise an army to attack the royalists in Acapulco. By the time Morelos was ready to march, two thousand men, Indians, blacks, and mestizos, had joined his company. After Hidalgo's execution on July 30, 1811, Morelos was committed to continuing the fight. In September of 1813, he arranged a meeting at Chilpancingo to put forth the necessity of selecting a leader. In less than an hour, Morelos was chosen and the next day announced his plan calling for the formation of a Mexican republic and total independence.

On November 6, 1813, this was formalized in a "Solemn Declaration of Independence of North America."[21] At this meeting, the newly installed congress voted in favor of a monthly pension of five hundred dollars to Leona as reward for her support. However, the insurgents needed this money to continue their fight and she received only one payment.[22]

Leona and Andrés Quintana Roo were married in 1814 at the insurgent camp. Now she was a fugitive like her husband, moving constantly, mostly on foot, and always in danger of falling into royalist hands. They were very poor and wandered through mountains and villages often in need of food and shelter. A reward for her capture made them a tempting target for betrayal. Leona was daring, a born freedom lover and patriot; she encouraged her husband to continue the fight when he weakened, never leaving his side.

Meanwhile, the Spanish government declared her an enemy of the country and confiscated her property in Mexico City. The Spanish viceroy intensified his attacks on the rebel forces, and the congress at Chilpancingo was forced to move several times until at last it dissolved. Following Morelos' capture, the War for Independence fell apart. The few members of the guerrilla bands holding out in the mountains, like Andrés and Leona, were all that remained of the first phase of the movement. After the execution of Morelos by firing squad in December of 1815, the royalists were close to victory and the first phase of the war ended.[23]

During the period of 1816 and 1817, lacking a leader to reunify the movement, the war was carried on by small guerrilla bands in the mountains of southern Mexico under the authority of local chiefs like Vicente Guerrero and Albino García. Neither the people nor the economy could stand more years of war, and they began to look for alternatives for gaining independence from Spain. Upon Napoleon's defeat in Spain, Ferdinand VII regained the throne and promised to liberalize his government. Fidelity to the king in Spain was particularly strong among the royalist armies in Mexico, composed largely of creoles, mestizos, blacks, and Indians. This factor and the conciliatory measures adopted by the viceroyship during these years placated some insurgents and were setbacks to the movement for independence.[24]

On January 3, 1817, in a cave at Achipixtla, Leona gave birth to their first daughter, Genoveva. Leona and Andrés were poor, tired of running, and sick of hiding. Carrying a child through the mountains and delivering it in the wilds had taken its toll on Leona. Quintana Roo worried that he would be unable to raise and educate their daughter. He left his family hoping by his absence to shield them from harm. But on March 18, 1818, Leona and her daughter were discovered hiding in a ravine near Tlacocuapa in the Tletlaya mountains and taken to San Pedro Tejupilco.

Andrés was misinformed about the treatment they received during the capture by the royalist army and hurried to surrender himself in exchange for their freedom. He renounced his liberal ideology and agreed to serve King Ferdinand VII. Leona received a pardon and the family was ordered to move to Spain. This order was eventually rescinded and they were directed to establish residence in Toluca. They would later be allowed to return to Mexico City.[25]

The final phase of the war took place from 1818 to 1821. Many liberal European politicians and intellectuals sympathized with the Mexican struggle for universal liberty. Just when all seemed lost, the government of Ferdinand VII was jeopardized by the liberal revolution in Spain. This deeply concerned the conservative elements in Mexico, including the church and large *haciendados*, who realized it was time for a change. They decided to support independence in their own way, resolve their differences with the people, bring an end to open hostilities, and unite under one flag.[26] A clash between the revolutionaries led by Vicente Guerrero and conservative forces under the leadership of Agustín de Iturbide was averted when the two men agreed to the independence of Mexico in 1821.[27]

Now it was time for Leona and Andrés to reap the benefits of independence. Andrés completed his law studies in the turmoil of newly independent Mexico City, and Iturbide named him under secretary of state and minister of internal and external affairs. Leona continued to speak out against injustice and championed causes of liberty. When her husband became disgusted with the imperialist ambitions of Iturbide, who had himself declared emperor, she encouraged Andrés to resign and they moved to Toluca to live in great deprivation.[28]

Early in the 1820s, Leona petitioned the Constitutional Convention for the return of her property as reparation for the losses she suffered during the insurrection. She was given a hacienda in Ocotepec in the plains of Apam and three houses. This allowed them to lead a better life. Her property in Mexico City was not returned, and she received no monetary compensation for the seizure of her goods while she was a fugitive.[29]

In 1823 a second daughter, María Dolores de la Soledad, was born. Leona raised their daughters and managed the hacienda. Andrés started a newspaper and continued his political activities, but he lacked the zeal of earlier years. He returned to the pleasures of literature and writing poetry. Fanny Calderón de la Barca, the Scottish wife of Spain's first minister to Mexico, wrote in a book first published in 1843 of her meeting with Andrés Quintana Roo: "[He] possesses all the calmness of a man whose first years have been spent in excitement and troubles, and who at length finds consolation in study alone...." She compared him to other men in Mexico who after years of taking an active role in the politics of their country, "...have seen the inutility of their efforts in favour of their country, and have now retreated into the bosom of their families, where they endeavor to forget public evils in domestic retirement and literary occupation."[30]

Quintana Roo continued to speak out against injustice. In 1830, writing in his newspaper, he attacked the policies of president Anastasio Bustamante. Bustamante ordered his arrest. Leona traveled to Mexico City to ask for bail from the president who had been a royalist and persecuted her in 1813. She was insulted by the *bustaministas*, particularly Lucas Alamán, minister of relations and also a writer. Bustamante agreed to release Andrés, but Leona refused to tolerate their outrageous behavior. In 1831 she courageously published a letter that exposed Alamán's conduct when she went to the national palace to see the president. From then on they were left in peace.

Leona dedicated the rest of her life to intellectual pursuits at her husband's side; she was exceedingly well educated for a woman of that era. She contributed articles to Andrés newspapers and helped with his political campaigns, suffering with him the problems of a public life.[31] Later the territory next to Yucatán was renamed "Quintana Roo" to honor him as a national hero.

Leona Vicario died on August 21, 1842, at her house in Mexico City, revered and admired by her countrymen as a heroine of Mexican independence.

NOTES ON CHAPTER FIVE

1. José María Miquel i Vergés, *Diccionario de insurgentes* (Mexico: Editorial Porrúa, 1969), 597; and Jonathan Kandell, *La Capital: The Biography of Mexico City* (New York: Random House, 1988), 282; and Perla Chinchilla Pawling, col., *Leona Vicario.* Serie de Cuadernos Conmemorativos, Comisión Nacional para las Celebraciónes del 175 Aniversario de la Independencia Nacional y 75 Aniversario de la Revolución Mexicana (Mexico: Instituto Nacional de Estudios Históricos de la Revolución Mexicana, Col. Juárez, C.P., 1985), 13-14.

2. C.A. Echánove-Trujillo, *Leona Vicario: La Mujer Fuerte de la Independencia,* (Mexico: Ediciones, Xochitl, 1945), 24-26.

3. Ibid., 27-28.

4. Chinchilla Pawling, col., *Leona Vicario,* 13; and Kandell, *La Capital: The Biography of Mexico City,* 282.

5. Morris Rosenblum, *Heroes of Mexico* (New York: Fleet Press Corporation, 1969), 72; and Chinchilla Pawling, col., *Leona Vicario,* 13-14; and Echánove-Trujillo, *Leona Vicario: La Mujer Fuerte de la Independencia,* 28-29; and Kandell, *La Capital: The Biography of Mexico City,* 282.

6. Carlos González Peña; Gusta Barfield Nance and Florene Johnson Dunstan, trs., *History of Mexican Literature: Third Edition* (Dallas: Southern Methodist Press, 1968), 176.

7. Ibid., 169.

8. Echánove-Trujillo, *Leona Vicario: La Mujer Fuerte de la Independencia,* 29-30.

9. Howard T. Fisher and Marion Hall Fisher, eds. and anns., *Life in Mexico: The Letters of Fanny Calderón de la Barca with New Material from the Author's Private Journals* (Garden City, New York: Doubleday & Company,

Inc., 1966), 765; and Kandell, *La Capital: The Biography of Mexico City*, 282-283.

10. Heriberto García Rivas, *Biografias de Mexicanos Ilustres* (Mexico: Grupo Editorial Diana, S.A., Universaro, 1962), 134.

11. González Peña, *History of Mexican Literature: Third Edition*, 176; and Chinchilla Pawling, col., *Leona Vicario*, 8.

12. Ibid., 9, 14; and Kandell, *La Capital: The Biography of Mexico City*, 283; and T.R. Fehrenbach, *Fire and Blood: A History of Mexico* (New York: Macmillan Publishing Co., Inc., 1973), 334; and González Peña, *History of Mexican Literature: Third Edition*, 169.

13. Chinchilla Pawling, col., *Leona Vicario*, 13; and Martha Cotera, *Profile on the Mexican American Woman* (Austin, Texas: National Educational Laboratory Publishers, Inc., 1976), 36, 40.

14. Chinchilla Pawling, col., *Leona Vicario*, 7-10.

15. Ibid., 25-26.

16. Ibid., 13-14; and Rosenblum, *Heroes of Mexico*, 73; and Kandell, *La Capital: The Biography of Mexico City*, 283.

17. Fisher and Fisher, eds. and anns., *Life in Mexico, The Letters of Fanny Calderón de la Barca*, 765.

18. Chinchilla Pawling, col., *Leona Vicario*, 14; and Miquel i Vergés, *Diccionario de insurgentes*, 597.

19. J.J. Fernández de Lizardi, *Heroinas mexicanas* (Mexico: Biblioteca de Historiadores Mexicanos, 1955), 9-10; and Chinchilla Pawling, col., *Leona Vicario*, 15; and Miquel i Verges, *Diccionario de insurgentes*, 597.

20. Chinchilla Pawling, col., *Leona Vicario*, 15; and García Rivas, *Biografias de Mexicanos Ilustres*, 134.

21. Bob and Jan Young, *Liberators of Latin America* (New York: Lothrop, Lee & Shephard Co., 1970), 166; and Irene Nicholson, *The Liberators: A Study of Independence*

Movements in Spanish America (New York, Washington: Frederick A. Praeger, Publishers, 1969), 246-247.

22. Chinchilla Pawling, col., *Leona Vicario*, 15.

23. Ibid., 7-8, 10.

24. Ibid., 10-11; and Young, *Liberators of Latin America*, 169, 170.

25. Chinchilla Pawling, col., *Leona Vicario*, 16; and García Rivas, *Biografias de Mexicanos Ilustres*, 135.

26. Chinchilla Pawling, col., *Leona Vicario*, 11; and W. Dirk Raat, ed., *Mexico: From Independence to Revolution, 1810-1910* (Lincoln and London: University of Nebraska Press, 1982), Octavio Paz, "The Meaning of Mexican Independence," 54.

27. Young, *Liberators of Latin America*, 176.

28. Miquel i Verges, *Diccionario de insurgentes*, 598; and Chinchilla Pawling, col., *Leona Vicario*, 16.

29. Ibid., 16; and García Rivas, *Biografias de Mexicanos Ilustres*, 135.

30. Fisher and Fisher, eds. and anns., *The Letters of Fanny Calderón de la Barca*, 421-422.

31. García Rivas, *Biografías de Mexicanos Ilustres*, 135.

CHAPTER SIX

Madam Candelaria
Mysterious Presence at the Alamo

One of the most colorful, albeit controversial, characters in the battle for Texas independence was a Mexican woman called Madam Candelaria. Until her death at the age of 113, this indomitable figure remained steadfast in her assertion that she attended James Bowie during his final days at the Alamo. She never tired of telling her stories to visitors, but, as happens with oft-told tales, there were misunderstandings and inconsistencies.

Her detractors were quick to point to these discrepancies, throwing doubt on the authenticity of her recollections. There was no confirmation of her presence at the Alamo by those who survived the attack. Some claimed it was only in her lively mind that these events took place. However, although no one would swear to the validity of her claim, no one could absolutely refute it either.

Much of what was known about Madam Candelaria came from direct interviews with the aging woman and her family. While this was subject to interpretation, certain facts remain to paint a fairly accurate portrait of the woman. That she was courageous, compassionate, and fiercely dedicated to the cause of freedom cannot be denied.

Andrea Castañon was born on November 30 or December 1, 1785. The dates vary as greatly as the location of her birth, which was reported to be in Presidio de Rio Grande, Mexico, Laredo, and San Juan Bautista. Several years before her death, in an endeavor to end speculation, her relatives in San Antonio obtained certification, recorded in the handwriting of a Catholic priest, establishing her birth at Presidio de Rio Grande in 1785. Unfortunately, this document was misplaced and there was no move to secure another.

Her father, Antonio Castañon, was a Spanish soldier, perhaps even an officer, who served in Cuba prior to his arrival at a Mexican garrison to fight the Indians. He also worked as a tailor for the Spanish King Ferdinand VII. Her mother, Francisca Ramírez, was Mexican.[1]

The family moved to Laredo when Andrea was three years old and then resettled in San Antonio de Bexar in 1810.[2] Andrea was then twenty-five, petite, dark, and comely like her mother. She recalled her employment as a servant for the wife of Don Manuel Antonio Cordero y Bustamante, the Spanish governor of Texas from 1805 to 1810. She was assigned to the kitchen and excelled as skilled cook and chocolate-maker.[3]

Andrea married Silberio Flores y Abrigo, a revolutionary who supported the ideologies of Father Miguel Hidalgo's independence movement, even after the priest's execution in 1811. In 1813 Silberio joined the Gutiérrez-Magee Expedition, which grew out of that movement. He was part of a sizeable force made up of Anglo-Americans, Mexicans, and Indians determined to end Spanish rule. However, they were greatly out-numbered and their

Madam Candelaria

McCullough Collection, The Daughters of the Republic of Texas Library at the Alamo.

attempt failed miserably. Silberio died in the bloody battle against the Spanish royalist forces under the command of Commandant-General Joaquín de Arredondo near the Medina River.

Two days later, Arredondo marched his troops into San Antonio de Bexar and imprisoned citizens suspected of revolutionary sympathies. He then ordered the arrest of the wives and female relatives of those men. Andrea was among those women imprisoned at a nearby estate known as *La Quinta*. For four months, they were forced daily to grind Indian corn and make tortillas for Arredondo's soldiers. The terrified women and girls were treated brutally until the army finally headed back to Mexico. After fifty-four days, Andrea was released to find her home looted, her possessions destroyed.[4]

The once-thriving city was now almost deserted, but its remaining residents were determined to rebuild. San Antonio began the slow return to normalcy; however, rough times were not over. Hostile Indians terrorized the small town. Food supplies were scarce and prices for available goods were high. Farmers worked their nearby lands with a plow in one hand, a rifle in the other.

Townspeople looking to the ragtag assignment of soldiers left for their protection found they were more trouble than their worth. The ill-equipped soldiers, often rowdy, were clearly displeased with this posting. Left with little to do, other than repelling occasional Indian attacks, they turned to gambling and drink to wile away long hours. Women feared the scurrilous soldiers almost as much they did the stray Indians riding breakneck through the dusty streets.[5]

Then in 1819, just as citizens were beginning to get a grip on their lives, the town was hit with torrential rains and devastated by flood waters, which claimed twenty-eight lives and demolished homes and businesses.[6] Andrea nursed the sick and consoled the families of the dead. She seemed to be everywhere with her curative soups and medicinal herbs. Rich or poor, they all needed her.

It was not until Mexican victory over Spanish rule in 1821, marking the beginning of the Republic of Texas, that San Antonio showed signs of full recovery. A large number of troops, smartly attired and better equipped, were stationed in the town and the economy, fueled by easier access to goods, prospered. Although still plagued by the random forays of Indians, particularly the Comanches, the town fought back with pride and determination. The population grew and soon it became necessary to build a schoolhouse for the Anglo-American children. In 1828 McClure's opened to educate the children of new settlers.[7]

Sometime in the 1830s, Andrea married Candelario Villanueva and after that became known as Madam Candelaria. She opened a small hotel near Alamo Plaza and quickly earned fame for cooking the best Mexican food in town. Her vivacious personality in addition to her culinary skill made her a success. Over the years she watched San Antonio grow from a small sleepy town of adobe houses and unpaved streets to a hub of excitement, and she was proud to be part of that excitement.[8]

By 1836 the people talked of nothing but independence. In homes and cafes, blacksmith shops and general stores, wherever men congregated they discussed plans to free Texas from Mexican domination. Indian fighters and soldiers, fresh from uprisings and skirmishes in other territories, traded stories with farmers and cattle drivers.

One of their favorite meeting places was the little hotel, not far from the Alamo, owned by the good-natured Mexican woman called Madam Candelaria. Many famous Americans and renowned Mexicans gathered at her tables to eat, sing, and swap tales. David Crockett, Sam Houston, Erasmo Seguin, José Antonio Navarro, Placido Benavides, and William B. Travis, leading supporters of the Texas Revolution, were welcomed at her hotel and in her home.[9]

Andrea hated the Mexican government and Antonio López de Santa Anna with good cause. Santa Anna had been a lieutenant in Joaquín de Arredondo's army of Spanish royalists at the Battle of Medina in 1813. She was well acquainted with his cruelty. More than eight hundred courageous men, including her first husband, were shot down and left dead or wounded on that battleground. Andrea was fiercely committed to the cause of freedom.[10]

Now, only three months after the Texans had sent General Martín Perfecto de Cós back toward Mexico in defeat,[11] the Alamo was being readied for battle. One hundred eighty-nine brave soldiers and civilians, armed only with swords, muskets, and cannon, stood ready to defend it against Santa Anna's army of three thousand.

At this time, Madam Candelaria received a personal letter from General Sam Houston, commander in chief of the Texan army. He asked her, as a favor to himself, to leave the safety of her hotel to nurse his friend, the adventurer and Indian fighter James Bowie. His symptoms resembled those of pleurisy, tuberculosis, or pneumonia. Houston was unaware of the exact nature of Bowie's illness, but he knew the man was gravely ill.

(Maurice Elfer in his 1933 published book, *Madam Candelaria: Unsung Heroine of the Alamo*, revealed that verification of Houston's letter came from a statement made to him in 1924 by James Villanueva, a grandson of the woman.)[12]

Upon receipt of General Houston's letter, Madam Candelaria joined the soldiers and the few civilians seeking protection at the Alamo and began nursing Bowie. She found him lying upon a narrow cot in a small room in the fort. The exact location of Bowie's position is questionable.[13] He was wasted from the fever and each breath was tortuous. A rifle and two pistols left by Colonel David Crockett were nearby.

Bowie and William Barrett Travis held joint command at the Alamo, but, while still officially second in command, Bowie was weak and not likely to recover. Lying on his cot, he watched Travis, known for his flair for the dramatic, draw a line with his sword on the earthen floor of the Alamo and heard him ask those prepared to give their lives for Texas to step over to join him. Sick as he was, Bowie matched his friend's fervor as he called out to have his cot carried over the line. Although she could not repeat Travis's exact words, Andrea quoted Bowie, "Boys, won't none of you help me over there?"[14]

In spite of the danger, she stayed by his side day and night throughout the thirteen-day siege, which began on February 23, 1836, ever mindful of her promise to Houston. From time to time, she raised Bowie's head giving him sips of water to relieve the incessant cough and bathed his head to bring down the fever. From her nursing experience during the flood of 1819, Andrea realized there was little she could do except offer whatever comfort possible to the man entrusted to her care.

Before daylight on March 6, they heard the bugles. A collective chill ran through the Alamo as the first notes of the *deguello* drifted over the mission walls. There was no doubting Santa Anna's intent: no quarter given, no prisoners taken. The first bugle's piercing notes, answered in turn by the blasting sounds from each unit as it prepared to attack, heralded the assault. Mexican commanders used more than fifty different bugle calls to give orders to their troops, but the *deguello* was the one most familiar and most feared. Taken from the Spanish, it literally meant beheading.[15]

The Mexican army, red flags flying, swelling to a force greater than three thousand, charged repeatedly. Those within the limestone walls of the fortress were vastly outnumbered, yet they fought bravely, aware there was little, if any, hope for reinforcements in response to Travis's letters or chance for survival against the frenzied attack. The soldiers finally burst through the gates of the Alamo, brutally hacking away with swords and bayonets at anyone alive, deaf to the cries from the wounded.

They discovered Bowie, Madam Candelaria at his side. Painfully raising himself from his cot with a final rush of courage, Bowie grabbed the pistols left within his reach by David Crockett and shot two of his attackers before his death. Andrea described the event:

> "I threw myself in front of him and received two bayonets in my body. One passed through my arm and the other through the flesh of my chin."

She paused to show her scars before continuing her story.

> "I implored them not to murder a sick man, but they thrust me out of the way and butchered my friend before my eyes.
> "All was silent now. The massacre had ended. One hundred and seventy-six of the bravest men the world ever saw had fallen and not one asked for mercy. I walked out of the cell, and when I stepped on the floor of the Alamo, the blood ran into my shoes."[16]

In a conflicting report, she said Bowie died at eleven o'clock the night just before the fall of the Alamo and that she was wounded while trying to shield his lifeless body from the bayonets of the Mexican soldiers. This story was heard first by her daughter or an adopted daughter and handed down to one of her grandsons.[17]

Bowie's body was added to the funeral pyres ordered by Santa Anna, joining those of the others who died defending the rights of independence. Three pyres were constructed, dry wood and brush alternating with layers of bodies. Later the bodies of Mexican soldiers were added. The smoke from the fires hovered over the Alamo for three weeks; the sight and smells remained with the people of Texas much longer.[18]

There were survivors who witnessed the slaughter: Susanna Dickinson, wife of Captain Almeron Dickinson, and her 15-month-old daughter, Angelina; Gertrudis Navarro, age 15, adopted sister of James Bowie's wife, Ursula; Juana Navarro Alsbury, Gertrudis' sister, and her 18-month-old son, Alijo; Ana, wife of Gregorio Esparza, and her four children: Enrique, Francisco, Manuel, and María de Jesus; William B. Travis' servant, Joe; Trinidad Saucedo; Petra Gonzales.[19]

In all, thirteen women and children who had sought safety within the Alamo walls were released by Mexican soldiers. Not one of them admitted to seeing Madam Candelaria. Did their own fears blind them to the presence of the small dark woman at the side of the fallen hero? Were they hiding in other locations, shielding themselves and their children? Were they resentful because of her Mexican heritage and discounted her contribution as nurse to Bowie? There were references to Mexican women walking out of the Alamo after the battle and some that stated there were more than thirteen, even as many as twenty-five, but Andrea Candelaria was never named.[20]

Leaving the Alamo under guard, Madam Candelaria was among the women set to caring for the wounded Mexican soldiers and was forced into hard labor as punishment for aiding the Texans.[21] It was then that her story became known and doubts about her actual presence within the fortress emerged. Each survivor was deluged with requests for a personal account of the siege and each account varied. Only hers was challenged. Perhaps Andrea Castañon Villanueva was caught up in Alamo fever; perhaps she was telling the truth.

Texas finally won its independence from Mexico in 1836 after Santa Anna's defeat at San Jacinto. Throughout the state, Texans celebrated. San Antonio came alive with its own special kind of celebration—the fandango, a reminder of earlier Castilian times. People danced in the streets to rousing music and came together to eat and revel at large parties.

Madam Candelaria was the undeniable leader of the fandangos.[22] Already famous for her Mexican food, she plunged into preparing sumptuous dishes for the crowds. Pungent aromas hung in the air around her cooking stove; sauces hot enough to blow smoke through your ears, some said, and she gloried in the crowd's delight. Using the chocolate-making techniques perfected as a servant girl, she created sweet confections to rival the sweetness of victory. Her small hotel was again a hive of activity, its tables overflowing with spicy foods to satisfy the revellers.

San Antonio gradually settled down after victory as people resumed the normal patterns of their lives and rebuilt homes and stores ransacked by the invaders. Andrea earned money cooking for the city's rich and famous inhabitants and used it to help the poor. When smallpox epidemics raged through the city, she was called upon to nurse the sick, and many grateful citizens were indebted to her care. She called on indefatigable inner resources to respond to the needs of the community while also caring for her own family.[23]

In September of 1842, Mexican General Adrian Woll took San Antonio in a surprise invasion. Candelario Villanueva was captured in the attack, and for three days Madam Candelaria supplied the captives with food. Later she contributed money for their aid when they were taken to Mexico as prisoners. As her husband was Mexican and not involved with the city's government, he was released.[24]

Andrea was blessed with a nurturing spirit. Whenever she learned of someone in trouble, she found a way to help. Often she gave away money and possessions she needed for herself. Not only did she raise four children of her own, three sons and a daughter, but she cared for twenty-two foster children. When one terribly abused youngster was brought to her attention by the Commissioner's Court, she insisted upon formally adopting the child.

Madam Candelaria talked freely about her experience at the Alamo. She was a firsthand witness to its bloody horrors. In an undated interview, reprinted from *The St. Louis Republic* and published by *The San Antonio Light* on February 19, 1899, she vividly described David Crockett as:

> "...one of the strangest men I ever saw. He had the face of a woman, and his manner was that of a girl. I could never regard him as a hero until I saw him die. He looked grand and terrible, standing at the front door and fighting a whole column of Mexican infantry. He had fired his last shot, and had not time to reload. The cannon balls had knocked away the sandbags and the infantry was pouring through the breach. Crockett stood there, swinging something over his head. The place was full of smoke and I could not tell whether he was using a gun or a sword. A heap of dead was piled at his feet, and the Mexicans were lunging at him with bayonets, but he would not retreat an inch. Poor Bowie could see it all, but he could not raise himself from his cot. Crockett fell and the Mexicans poured into the Alamo."[25]

She told of seeing Santa Anna in the streets of San Antonio, disguised as a mule driver selling hay, and thought then that he was laying his battle plans. She reminisced about the men who dined at her tables. Newspaper reporters and curious visitors from all over the world came for interviews or to just listen to her stories about the historic changes she witnessed during her lifetime.

Andrea had an excellent memory and delighted in regaling visitors with her tales and answering their questions. She happily sat for souvenir photographs. In pictures taken late in her life, she posed with her Mexican hairless dog either in her lap or at her feet. She believed the animal was a cure for her rheumatism.[26]

Not everyone believed in the authenticity of her recollections. Detractors found marked discrepancies in her stories, and there was no confirmation of her presence at the Alamo by those who also survived the attack. However, neither could anyone absolutely prove she was not at the fort.[27]

Several leading citizens of San Antonio called for final disposition of this matter before death claimed the woman who was now more than one hundred years old. A petition was signed on March 25, 1889, requesting the legislature to bestow a pension upon Madam Candelaria in recognition of her service and loyalty during the revolution. Old Texas soldiers testified that she saved the lives of many persons who were in danger of execution by Santa Anna's forces. On February 12, 1891, the Alamo Monument Association announced that it had thoroughly checked her story and was satisfied of her presence at the Alamo throughout the course of the siege.

On April 13, 1893, the twenty-second legislature of the Texas House and Senate, sitting in regular session in the city of Austin, passed an act granting Madam Candelaria a pension "in recognition and as a reward for service rendered by her as nurse during the siege of the Alamo, at the rate of one hundred and fifty dollars per year." This came almost too late to be of great financial help to the poor woman but, nevertheless, must have brought some vindication of the slights suffered over the years.[28]

At that time, she was living in a small cottage at 611 Laredo Street. She still received visitors and was assisted by a Spanish-speaking girl who stayed at her side. Her eyesight failed about three years before her death, but this did not diminish her enjoyment in talking about early San Antonio, wild fandangos, and, of course, the final days of Jim Bowie. Even toward the end, blind, speaking with great effort in a halting English, and slipping into the Spanish of her childhood, she fascinated visitors by her remarkably picturesque monologues.

During February of 1899, she became gravely ill and it was apparent she would not live long. The night before her death, extremely weak and barely able to speak, she told her family she was ready for death to end her suffering.

On February 10, at 2:20 p.m., Andrea Castañon Candelaria Villanueva, the last survivor of the Alamo, died of complications of influenza. She was 113 years old. Her final home was with her daughter Francisca Flores Pacheo, at 419 South Concho Street. She was survived by two children and four grandchildren.

The San Antonio *Daily Express* of Saturday, February 11, 1899, reported that her body, laid out upon a white-draped stretcher, was dressed in a brown St. Francis scapular-type shroud, trimmed at the neck and sleeves with white lace, a satin ribbon at the waist. Funeral services were held in the cathedral of San Fernando at 9:30 on the morning following her death. She was buried in the San Fernando cemetery.

Citizens of San Antonio shared fond memories of the colorful woman. Some recalled her generosity to the stranded families of the forty-niners who passed through the city on their way to the California gold mines. Many spoke of her care of orphaned children she treated as her own.

Andrea supported the cause of freedom all her life. She even sent small amounts of money in care of the Cuban junta in New York. Once, after receiving her pension check, she was about to send her granddaughter to the store to buy shoes she needed for herself. Then she heard something about Cuba.

"Never mind the shoes, send the two dollars to the Cubans. I can go barefooted until next pay day," she was reported to say.[29]

Yet for all her good deeds, Madam Candelaria remained best remembered for the controversy surrounding her presence at the Alamo, the story she told until she could speak no more.

NOTES ON CHAPTER SIX

1. Maurice Elfer, *Madam Candelaria: Unsung Heroine of the Alamo* (Houston, Texas: The Rein Company, Publishers, 1933; reprint courtesy of the Daughters of the Republic of Texas Library at the Alamo), 18; and Crystal Sasse Ragsdale, *The Women and Children of the Alamo*, (Austin, Texas: State House Press, 1994), 41.

2. Elfer, *Madam Candelaria: Unsung Heroine of the Alamo,* 18.

3. Ragsdale, *The Women and Children of the Alamo,* 41.

4. Ibid., 43; and Boyce House, *San Antonio: City of Flaming Adventure* (San Antonio, Texas: The Naylor Company, 1968), 22-23; and Ted Schwarz, *Forgotten Battlefield of the First Texas Revolution: The Battle of Medina, August 18, 1813,* (Austin, Texas: Eakin Press, 1985), 108-110.

5. House, *San Antonio: City of Flaming Adventure,* 26-27.

6. Ragsdale, *The Women and Children of the Alamo,* 44; and House, *San Antonio: City of Flaming Adventure,* 27.

7. Ragsdale, *The Women and Children of the Alamo,* 43-44; and House, *San Antonio: City of Flaming Adventure,* 33-34.

8. Ragsdale, *The Women and Children of the Alamo,* 44.

9. Daniel James Kubiak, *Ten Tall Texans* (San Antonio, Texas: The Naylor Company, 1970), 74; and Ragsdale, *The Women and Children of the Alamo,* 44.

10. Elfer, *Madam Candelaria: Unsung Heroine of the Alamo,* 9.

11. Alwyn Barr, *Texans in Revolt: The Battle for San Antonio, 1835* (Austin: University of Texas Press, 1990), 58-59; and Walter Lord, *A Time to Stand* (New York: Harper & Row, Publishers, 1961), 57.

12. Elfer, *Madam Candelaria: Unsung Heroine of the Alamo,* 8.

13. Lord, *A Time to Stand,* 205.

14. Elfer, Maurice, "Madame Candelaria, Unsung Heroine of the Alamo Nursed Bowie to the End" (Dallas, Texas: *The Dallas Morning News*, Sunday, March 9, 1930).

15. Richard G. Santos, *Santa Anna's Campaign Against Texas, 1835-1836, Featuring the Field Commands Issued to Major General Vicente Filisola* (Salisbury, North Carolina: Texian Press, 1968), 36.

16. Elfer, "Madame Candelaria, Unsung Heroine of the Alamo Nursed Bowie to the End."

17. Ibid.

18. Santos, *Santa Anna's Campaign Against Texas, 1835-1836*, 77.

19. The Daughters of the Republic of Texas present "The story of The Alamo: Thirteen fateful days in 1836," unpaged.

20. R.M. Potter, *The Fall Of The Alamo: A Reminiscence of the Revolution of Texas* (San Antonio: Herald Steam Press, 1860. Reprinted by Fuller Printing Company, Bryan, Texas, 1979), 12, reference to "another Mexican woman"; and Reuben M. Potter, *The Fall of The Alamo*, Introduction and Notes by Charles Grosvenor (Hillsdale, New Jersey: The Otterden Press, 1977), 38, reference to "a few Mexican women with their children"; and Santos, *Santa Anna's Campaign Against Texas, 1835-1836*, 76, "Some 15 to 25 people, mainly women and children related to the Alamo defenders, survived the siege and assault of the fortress."; and Lord, *A Time to Stand*, 207-208, stated there were fourteen survivors, but that Madam Candelaria was not among them.

21. Ragsdale, *The Women and Children of the Alamo*, 48.

22. House, *San Antonio: City of Flaming Adventure*, 164.

23. "The Last Voice Hushed: Death of Madam Candelaria Yesterday," San Antonio *Daily Express*, Saturday morning, February 11, 1899, reprint courtesy of the

Daughters of the Republic of Texas Library at the Alamo.

24. Ragsdale, *The Women and Children of the Alamo*, 50.

25. Elfer, *Madam Candelaria: Unsung Heroine of the Alamo*, 14-15.

26. "The Last Voice Hushed: Death of Madam Candelaria Yesterday," San Antonio *Daily Express*, Saturday morning, February 11, 1899; and Elfer, "Madam Candelaria, Unsung Heroine of the Alamo Nursed Bowie to the End," *The Dallas Morning News*, Sunday, March 9, 1930.

27. Susan Prendergast Schoelwer with Tom W. Glaser, *Alamo Images: Changing Perceptions of a Texas Experience* (Dallas, Texas: The DeGolyer Library and Southern Methodist University Press, 1985), 121.

28. From reprints courtesy of the Daughters of the Republic of Texas Library at the Alamo; and Elfer, *Madam Candelaria: Unsung Heroine of the Alamo*, 21.

29. Ibid., quoting San Antonio *Daily Express*; and Elfer, 21-22.

Francisca Alvarez
The Angel of Goliad

For almost a century the tale of Francisca "Panchita" Alvarez, the woman who bravely defied the orders of the Mexican command to execute all prisoners captured in the Texas Revolution, remained unchanged.[1] She had ridden out of Matamoros on February 18, 1836, at the side of Captain Telesforo Alvarez. Alvarez, from Toluca, was paymaster of the 6th Company of General José Urrea's cavalry regiment of Cuautla, which numbered almost one thousand men. He began his military career in 1821 as a private in the Mexican National Army and progressed smoothly through the ranks earning praise for distinguished service along the way. The army was now headed into Texas under the authority of General Antonio López de Santa Anna to put down the revolutionary colonists.[2]

It was generally believed that Alvarez met the young woman before leaving camp at Matamoros. They had stopped for the night, an army of regular soldiers, raw recruits, and muleteers, all hot and tired from the march.

Panchita was small, slim, and beautiful; she stood out against the backdrop of camp followers who were busy preparing the evening meal as the sun slowly sank beneath the horizon and the dust settled. It did not take long for the thirty-four-year-old Alvarez, handsome and self-assured, to convince the lovely señorita to accompany him as his wife. His legitimate wife in Toluca was of no concern. Alvarez was legally married to María Agustina de Pozo, but had abandoned her and their two children in 1834. Three years later, she and her brother wrote several letters to the minister of war requesting money for the support of her young family. There is no record of a response.[3]

Although Panchita possessed considerable physical charms, it may have been something else that captured the captain's attention. A streak of independence and a no-nonsense attitude distanced her from the women who typically followed the soldiers: the women who cooked their meals, did their laundry, nursed their ills, and warmed their beds until tossed aside when another caught their fancy. These were the women who walked for miles while their men often rode in carts or on horseback, women and children adding a dusty tail to the main body of troops.[4]

That Panchita was not an ordinary "camp wife" was also apparent to the men watching her ride into camp at Copano on March 27, 1836, at the side of a captain of the Mexican detachment. She rode at the front of the line, not in the rear with the weary followers. She carried herself as one accustomed to attracting the attention of men, yet her dark eyes missed nothing of the squalor of the encampment.

Reining her horse to an abrupt halt, she exploded into a torrent of Spanish upon discovering Major William P. Miller and his seventy-five volunteers, their arms numb from being bound so tightly that the flow of blood was

Francisca Alvarez, the Angel of Goliad

Bust at Presidio la Bahia. Photo by Dorothy Simmons.

111

restricted. She demanded their immediate release, ordering the ropes removed and that they be given water and food.[5]

Miller and his recruits from Nashville, Tennessee, had landed at Copano Bay on March 23 as reinforcements for the Legion of Texas Cavalry[6] and were forced to surrender without resistance before unloading their arms and ammunition. The grateful young men murmured their thanks through parched lips as Panchita Alvarez walked among them bringing water, using her *rebozo* to wipe the sweat from their eyes.

Next she moved to convince Colonel Francisco Garay, the officer in charge of the camp, to disobey Santa Anna's order of immediate execution since these men were not armed when captured and had not begun unloading supplies.[7] Flush with power after the massacre at the Alamo, Santa Anna had issued an order to his troops to proceed with the annihilation of the Texan rebels and the execution of all prisoners. Volunteers from most of the southern and a handful of the northern states, and several foreign countries, had eagerly joined the battle for freedom.[8] But to Santa Anna, they were all Texans and subject to his wrath. Garay was fully aware of the decisiveness of Santa Anna's decree and, although not in accord with its brutality, would not have challenged it. However, charmed by the impassioned plea from the captain's beautiful companion, it was not difficult to postpone this order. After all, if execution became necessary, it could be accomplished at Goliad where hundreds of soldiers awaited death. Major Miller's men were granted a reprieve.[9]

An earlier report of Panchita's compassion came from an event occurring the first week in March at San Patricio. There she found young Reuben Brown from Georgia about to be executed. Brown, one of Dr. James Grant's men on a mission to procure horses for a raid into Mexico, had been captured by General Urrea. The boy, luckier than those killed before they could escape, was caught by a lasso, then tied to a horse and taken to San Patricio where he was confined in a small hut for a week. Panchita threw herself between the youth and his executioner, then she and an unnamed priest pleaded for his life. Brown later confirmed this in a written account of his narrow escape: "I was then taken out to be shot, but was spared through the interposition of a Mexican lady, named Alvarez."[10]

Meanwhile, Colonel James Walker Fannin, stationed at Goliad, had been unable to respond to William B. Travis's call for immediate assistance at the Alamo, which he received on February 25, 1836. In a letter to his father, Fannin wrote of his troop's inexperience, the scarcity of provisions and ammunition, even their lack of suitable clothing, and compared them unfavorably to Santa Anna's army.[11]

Although Fannin and his men finally attempted to reach the Alamo, a series of mishaps aborted the undertaking and they returned to La Bahia, the fort at Goliad.

The presidio and mission of *La Bahia del Espiritu Santo* were founded by the Spaniards and settled permanently at Goliad in 1749. The Mexicans called it the "Fort of the Bay of the Holy Cross." To the men in Fannin's guard it was "La Bahia." Fannin, on the other hand, named the rebuilt garrison "Fort Defiance." He was convinced of its strategic importance as a supply center and for the relocation of troops, as well as for its position overlooking the seacoast at the juncture of Aransas Inlet and Matagorda Bay.[12]

Fannin received General Sam Houston's final order to move his men from Goliad to Victoria within a week after the fall of the Alamo. However, Fannin was reluctant to abandon the fortress, and his poorly organized retreat did not begin until March 19. He then compounded a series of judgmental errors by resting his troops and allowing their animals to graze and water in the middle of a prairie. This left them exposed and without defense against the attack from Urrea's cavalry at the Battle of Coleto. He also ignored the advice of Dr. Jack Shackelford, captain of a company from north Alabama called the Red Rovers, and others to press forward to the safety of the nearby woods.[13]

Urrea's troops overtook Fannin's meager force of three hundred on the open prairie. Fannin's men were surrounded, cut off from the protection of the woods to their north and without food or water. Refusing to abandon their wounded that night in order to save themselves, they were easy targets for Urrea's heavier artillery, which appeared accompanied by more troops before dawn. Rather than face certain death, Fannin, after a hasty meeting with his officers, raised a white flag and surrendered to Urrea. The terms of surrender, he explained to his men, assured them liberty without retribution. It offered the only hope for saving the wounded.[14]

Those who could walk were marched back to Goliad under tight guard and herded into the small chapel where they remained the night without food or water. Indeed, it was well into the second day before they were fed. The air in the chapel, heated by the bodies of so many, was stagnant and foul. There was precious little room for the exhausted men to lie down, and a parading guard took additional space. Sitting on the airless floor brought little relief and was only done for short periods, often as a last resort before collapse.[15]

The wounded were carted in the following day. At that time, the others were released from the confining walls of the church, which was too small for all the men and the wounded. The chapel then became the hospital. This change brought little relief as they were still hungry and wet from unremitting cold rain. Prisoners with a few gold coins or other valuables in their pockets bought scraps of food from soldiers or their women. A few days later Fannin's men were joined by Major Miller's force from

Copano, and on March 25, Colonel Ward and his captured soldiers were added.[16]

It was at this point that Second Sgt. Isaac D. Hamilton, a young volunteer from Alabama and member of Shackelford's Red Rovers captured at Coleto, first saw Panchita Alvarez. Hamilton watched in astonishment as a beautiful Mexican woman on horseback stopped not far from where he stood. Dismounting, she spoke a few words to the guards before entering the chapel to see the wounded Texans. She wasted no time. She ordered water for the suffering men, checked the dressings on their wounds, and eased them to more comfortable positions where they lay chilled on the damp ground.

"She's the 'Angel'," Hamilton heard one of Miller's young soldiers from Copano say. Little did he suspect that, like many others, he would owe his life to her and survive to tell the story. Miller's men, heartened by her appearance, shared their experiences with the "Angel." Their tales buoyed the spirits of the prisoners who had no idea their situation was hopeless. After dispensing the little aid she could to the wounded, Panchita approached the fort's commander. Colonel Nicolas de la Portilla looked up from the two dispatches on his desk. One from General Urrea advised him to keep the prisoners busy rebuilding the town and putting up a fort. It said to treat them well. Urrea had no taste for blood, unless he was particularly aroused. It was the second dispatch that alarmed him.[17]

It came from Santa Anna, dated March 23, 1836, and stated "that all foreigners taken with arms in their hands, making war upon the nation, shall be treated as pirates..." and ordered execution of these enemies of Mexico.[18]

The letter, delivered by express courier, arrived at seven o'clock the evening of the 26th. It was direct, but did not address the problem of Major Miller's men who were unarmed when captured. Portilla immediately sent word to Urrea to take the matter of Miller's men out of his hands. He was furious that he had been left at Goliad by Urrea to oversee the slaughter.

Now to further complicate his life, here was this woman not just pleading for mercy, but demanding it. Portilla was not a cruel man, he explained, just following orders. He listened as she spoke persuasively. Many prisoners had skills needed by the Mexican army. There were doctors, nurses, wheelwrights, blacksmiths. Surely these men could be spared, she reasoned. Others were hidden in her tent.[19]

The next morning was Palm Sunday, seven days since Fannin's surrender at Coleto. A heavily armed Mexican guard grouped the prisoners into three columns and marched them away from camp along three different roads. Some of the wounded were carried. Until this time, most of these men believed they would be freed under the terms of surrender signed by Fannin. The day preceding the massacre, anticipating reunion with their families, the men sang out merrily, "Home, Sweet, Home." However, Fannin was betrayed by the false conditions on the surrender. These stated each man would be treated in accordance with accepted civilized practices in dealing with prisoners of war and that within eight to ten days they would be sent to New Orleans or the closest port for repatriation to the United States. Fannin's small company made up in determination and grit what they lacked in numbers. They would have fought to the end rather than surrender to death by firing squad.[20]

Standing against the wall of the small chapel that had housed the wounded, Panchita sobbed bitterly. Her long black hair floated behind her as she paced, crying wildly, "Curse you, Santa Anna." She blamed herself. If only she had known earlier about the Palm Sunday execution, she might have been able to warn them or save more. Men, convinced they were on their way home, shouted out their thanks. They wondered why she wept. As the columns passed, she darted into their ranks and threw her arms around a boy, begging for his life. Fifteen-year-old Benjamin Franklin Hughes was spared by Colonel José Holsinger, who earlier, in an attempt to allay the Texans' apprehensions, had remarked to the prisoners of their release and liberty in "eight days."[21]

Forty years after that morning, Hughes wrote of his experience at Goliad. This record was preserved in the archives of the University of Texas among the Philip C. Tucker Papers. Hughes stated that standing among an unspecified number of women were the wife of General Urrea and "a young lady, Madame Captain Alvarez." Following an exchange of words between the two women, Hughes was separated from the other prisioners as "the rest marched off."[22]

Each unit of prisoners was escorted to a backdrop of brush and halted. Not before the Mexican guards turned to rejoin their ranks did the prisoners realize they had marched to their death. The slaughter stunned even the Mexicans with its brutality, yet they were driven to complete the job with guns, bayonets, and swords.[23]

Panchita had managed to save two surgeons: Dr. Jack Shackelford and Dr. Joseph H. Barnard. Eighteen other men with skills considered useful to the Mexican army also escaped execution that day. Among these were listed two hospital attendants and two carpenters. When she learned afterwards that Dr. Shackelford's son and two nephews were executed, she cried, "Why did I not know that you had a son here? I would have saved him at all hazards." From this statement, it is apparent she had no prior knowledge of the planned execution.[24]

Others were saved by dealings with officers who entered the fort at night and took them out to be hidden until after the massacre. A few managed by their own wits and daring to escape during the confusion. In the end, three-hundred fighting men and fifty wounded were killed. Major Miller's men, identifiable by white arm bands, were not harmed.[25]

Isaac D. Hamilton was one survivor. Although wounded in the right leg by gunshot and the left leg by bayonet thrust, he ran. Plunging over the low barricade, he remained hidden in tall prairie grass and later joined three others who were not wounded in the sheltering trees beyond. Zachariah Brooks, Dillard Cooper, and Wilson Simpson, from Isaac's company of Red Rovers, had also escaped. For more than a week, the three men alternately dragged and carried their wounded friend. Eleven days after the massacre, he agreed it was best for his companions to go on without him. His wounds were not healing; he was near death. They could probably save themselves without the burden of his extra weight to carry. Hamilton, starved and often delirious, survived by eating grass, wild onions, and elm buds. He fed off the rancid flesh remaining on beeves slaughtered by Mexican soldiers; he devoured a few ears of corn, raw fish, and a dove he caught.[26]

On April 14, returning to a riverbank for fish, Hamilton found a canoe and paddle submerged in the water. Giddy from this discovery, hidden as if by an unseen benefactor, he dared to hope he might reach safety. He paddled to Dimitt's Point, but when he left the water to search for food in a deserted town, he was spotted by Don Placido Benavides from Victoria. At the end of his strength, Hamilton did not attempt to escape. Benavides, once a leading Mexican supporter of independence, had been one of Dr. Grant's men; he had escaped capture and headed toward Goliad to warn Fannin of Urrea's advance.[27]

Benavides remembered Isaac Hamilton as the quartermaster of Shackelford's unit. He secretly continued to support the revolution, but worried about compromising his own family's safety by harboring the man. Even as he helped Isaac into his cart, he decided that if approached by a Mexican patrol, he would turn him over as an escaped prisoner. When Benavides was overtaken by lancers, he coldly betrayed Isaac, leaving him to his fate. The young man was put on a horse, which was whipped into a gallop, and, after a painful eighteen-mile ride, he arrived at Victoria.[28]

It was nineteen days after the massacre when Panchita discovered the terribly wounded man at Mexican headquarters in Victoria. Captain Alvarez and a small force were assigned to Victoria while Urrea marched ahead. Dr. Barnard confirmed her presence at Victoria in his journal: "She afterward showed much attention and kindness to the surviving prisoners, frequently sending messages and supplies of provisions to them from Victoria."[29]

There were other references to the presence of the "Angel," one from R.L. Owens, grandson of the Quinn family, one of three Irish-Texan families who remained in Victoria when it was occupied by Urrea. Owens recalled mention of "the wives of several Mexican officers" who interceded for a few Americans and saved them from the firing squad.[30]

After the horrors of Goliad, this was a pleasant respite for Panchita. She understood killing was a part of war and knew in her heart she had done what she could. Still the bloody scenes and heart-wrenching screams of the men played repeatedly in her mind. While taking a walk not far from camp, she unexpectedly came upon soldiers using Isaac for a horse to haul water from a river. He was hungry, feverish, and crippled with pain from his barely treated wounds. The soldiers laughed as they whipped him. Isaac strained at his ropes, making little progress and resulting in more lashings. Panchita ran to Alvarez begging him to stop this outrage. It was not difficult to give in to her pleading when she argued that Santa Anna had not ordered executions at Victoria. The prisoner could very well join the others being marched back to Goliad to be killed there, she said. Alvarez called for Isaac's release and assigned him to other camp chores until he regained strength. In affidavits dated at Houston, January 8, 1852, and at Galveston, January 28, 1858, Hamilton referred to two Mexican officers' wives.[31] The second woman in these and other references apparently did not make as great an impression on the young soldiers as did the wife of Captain Alvarez.

Panchita hurried back to the riverbank to check on Isaac and found him flat on his back. A Mexican soldier stood above him holding a dagger at his throat. As she cried out, the soldier, aware of the folly of crossing the captain's woman, released his grip on Isaac and stalked off. She knew he would be back with friends to kill the young American. Panchita took advantage of the confusion when news of the Mexican defeat at the San Jacinto River reached camp. The Mexican soldiers, crazed with hatred after receiving the news of Santa Anna's defeat and capture, would slaughter the prisoners. Enlisting the help of a sympathetic soldier, she lost no time plotting Isaac's escape. Then she informed him of the plan.

That same day, as Isaac appeared to be resting at the riverbank, a rough-looking soldier loudly ordered him to bring in the cows grazing not far away. To add substance to his command, the soldier kicked the young man as he began to rise from the ground. Isaac headed toward the cows and found the horse Panchita had hidden among the trees. He gratefully seized this opportunity for escape. Several soldiers saw Isaac ride off and gave chase, shooting as they rode. Isaac rode furiously for his life, kicking the horse without mercy and outdistancing his pursuers. He reached safety and found his way back to his mother's home in Courtland, Alabama, to recover from his wounds and the horrors of war. Thoughts of the lovely Panchita never left him; she became an obsession. She had told him to do a kindness in her name as repayment. Perhaps it was this that caused him to set free a slave named Maria. This act was recorded in the courthouse of Harris County, Texas, on February 26, 1841. The woman was twenty-five, about the same age as Panchita.

Hamilton suffered from a wanderlust after his return from battle and was barely able to support himself as a trader. He traveled to Arkansas, Louisiana, and to Houston and Galveston in Texas. He crossed South Texas and rode into Mexico searching for news of Panchita. He learned nothing and never saw her again. In 1858 the Texas Legislature, acting on a request to bring relief to the penniless survivor of the massacre, granted him land, a league in the vicinity of Beaumont. He died in 1859 before reaching it.[32]

Others also looked for the girl; her dark piercing eyes, her beauty and quiet dignity were unforgettable. They owed their lives to her defiant stand against the brutality of her countrymen. Throwing personal safety aside, she put herself at risk to aid the captured Texans, managing to save many. What prompted her response to these men, some of them not out of their teens? Was there something in her life, a life she never revealed, an unexpected gift of mercy she wished in some way to repay, that stirred her heart?

Following Mexico's defeat at San Jacinto, conditions at Victoria quickly deteriorated. Captain Alvarez, left in charge of the fort, lacked the experience to keep the men in line. The Mexican soldiers walked away from their duties. Countless deserted.[33]

Panchita returned to Matamoros with Alvarez and, in the summer of 1836, he abandoned her in Mexico City.[34] Perhaps it was time to go back to his wife; perhaps he tired of her. The correct spelling of her last name remains in question: Alinez, Alavez, Alevesco, Alvarez.[35]

Dr. Shackelford left Texas and returned to his home in Courtland, Alabama. Reuben Brown became a Texas planter and a colonel in the Confederate army. Benjamin F. Hughes sailed the seas as a sailor and U.S. Marine and died in Dallas at the age of seventy-five. Dr. J.H. Barnard settled in Goliad as a surveyor and served terms as a member of the Texas Legislature. He died in Canada while on a visit to his old home.[36]

Dr. Barnard kept a diary of his time as a volunteer during the Texan revolt against Mexico. First published in the *Goliad Guard* in 1883, it gave a firsthand account of the "Angel" and brought to light much of Panchita's story. After describing the events of March 27, 1836, he wrote:

"I must not here omit to mention Sinora Alinez, whose name ought to be prepetutated [sic] to the latest times for her virtues, and whose action contrasted so strangely with those of her countrymen, deserves to be recorded in the annals of this county and treasured in the heart of every Texan."

He added that upon her return to Matamoros, on her own and needy, she aided Americans imprisoned there and found refuge with friends and supporters who knew of her brave deeds.

"Her name deserves to be recorded in letters of gold among those angels who have from time to time been commissioned by an overruling and beneficent Power to relieve the sorrows and cheer the hearts of man, and who have for that purpose assumed the form of helpless woman, that the benefits of the boon might be enhanced by the strong and touching contrast of aggravated evils worked by friends in human shape, and balm poured on the wounds they make by a feeling and pitying woman."[37]

Captain Jack Shackelford also left his impression of Panchita:

> "I consider it not inappropriate here to mention one female, Pacheta Alevesco; the wife of Captain A. She was indeed an angel of mercy—a second Pocahontas. All that she could do to administer to our comfort,—to pour "oil into our wounds," was done. She had likewise been to Major Miller and men, a "ministering angel."[38]

Then, just as the history books had closed the chapter on the "Angel of Goliad," new information was uncovered. Among papers housed in the Texas State Archives belonging to Judge Harbert Davenport, there appeared a revealing story written in 1936 by Elena Zamora O'Shea of Dallas, Texas, a teacher on the Santa Gertrudis Division of the King Ranch during the 1902-1903 school year. She recalled one of the Mexican workers on the ranch, Don Matías Alvarez, the son of Panchita and Telesforo Alvarez. After hearing the tale of the Goliad Massacre read by Mrs. O'Shea from Mrs. Pennybacker's *History of Texas*, he questioned the omission of certain material.

Mrs. O'Shea's story went on to relate the information told to her by Don Matías. He said his father had been forced into an arranged marriage, but had only loved Panchita. The young lovers knew the Catholic church would not sanction annulment of his first union and decided to leave together when he was sent to Matamoros. Upon the war's end, they returned to Matamoros and had two children, the surviving one was Matías, and lived together until the death of Telesforo. It was Matías who brought Doña Panchita to the King Ranch with his family. Today there are several Alvarez descendants contributing to the welfare of the state.[39]

Within Judge Davenport's papers in the archives, a note written by Father Joseph G. O'Donohoe "made in complement of a letter which appeared on the editorial page of the *Dallas News*, Sunday, March 15, 1936" added to Mrs. O'Shea's account. Father O'Donohoe revealed that Panchita, who came from a good background, was orphaned early in her childhood and raised to become a "better class servant" by a prosperous family in the vicinity of San Luis Potosi.

He wrote that she knew of Telesforo's marriage, but "longing to be free and to have a fling at life, succumbed to the attentions of the dashing Captain, and throwing all restraint aside" accompanied him to Texas.

Father O'Donohoe's letter confirmed her death when she was in her nineties and her burial in an unmarked grave on the King Ranch.[40]

All that remains of Francisca Alvarez, the only person on the Mexican side of the battle for Texas independence to be honored by the state, is a carved figure at Presidio la Bahia. It stands in memory of her courage and mercy during a two-month period in Texas history, March to May 1836. She left an indelible mark on the hearts of Texas citizens.

NOTES ON CHAPTER SEVEN

1. Bill and Marjorie K. Walraven, *The Magnificent Barbarians: Little Told Tales of the Texas Revolution* (Austin, Texas: Eakin Press, 1993), 91.

2. Kathryn Stoner O'Connor, *The Presidio La Bahia del Espritu Santo de Zuniga 1721 to 1846* (Austin, Texas: Von Boeckmann-Jones Co., 1966), 271; and "The Angel of Goliad," Texas State Archives (Austin, Texas: Texas State Library).

3. O'Connor, *The Presidio La Bahia del Espritu Santo de Zuniga 1721 to 1846*, 273; and "The Angel of Goliad," Texas State Archives.

4. Elizabeth Salas, *Soldaderas in the Mexican Military: Myth and History* (Austin: University of Texas Press, 1990), 11.

5. J.A. White, ed., *Dr. J.H. Barnard's Journal, From December, 1835, to March 27th, 1836, Giving an Account of Fannin Massacre,* (Goliad, Texas: *Goliad Advance*, 1912), reproduced by J.A. White Family, 1988), 26-27. Courtesy of Goliad Chamber of Commerce.

6. Walter Prescott Webb, ed., *The Handbook of Texas* (Austin: The Texas State Historical Association, 1952), 701.

7. Lester Hamilton, *Goliad Survivor: Isaac D. Hamilton,* (San Antonio, Texas: The Naylor Company, 1971), 48.

8. Nell White, *Goliad in the Texas Revolution,* A Thesis Presented to the Faculty of the Graduate School University of Houston, May, 1941, (Austin, Texas: Eakin Publications Inc., 1988), 34-35. Courtesy of Goliad Chamber of Commerce.

9. Hamilton, *Goliad Survivor: Isaac D. Hamilton*, 48-49.

10. O'Connor, *The Presidio La Bahia del Espritu Santo de Zuniga 1721 to 1846,* 195; and *The Texas Almanac for 1859 with Statistics, Historical & Biographical Sketches &C. Relating to Texas* (Galveston: Richardson & Co.), 136.

11. Nell White, *Goliad in the Texas Revolution*, 38.

12. Webb, ed., *The Handbook of Texas*, 700, 701; and Hamilton, *Goliad Survivor: Isaac D. Hamilton*, 16.

13. Jakie L. Pruett and Everett B. Cole, Sr., *Goliad Massacre: A Tragedy of the Texas Revolution* (Austin, Texas: Eakin Press, 1985), 67-68, 78.

14. Webb, ed., *The Handbook of Texas*, 702-703; and Pruett and Cole, Sr., *Goliad Massacre: A Tragedy of the Texas Revolution*, 81-89.

15. Ibid., 98.

16. J.A. White, ed., *Dr. J.H. Barnard's Journal From December, 1835, to March 27th, 1836, Giving an Account of Fannin Massacre*, 22-23.

17. Hamilton, *Goliad Survivor: Isaac D. Hamilton*, 47, 49.

18. Pruett and Cole, Sr., *Goliad Massacre: A Tragedy of the Texas Revolution*, 105-106.

19. Hamilton, *Goliad Survivor: Isaac D. Hamilton*, 49; and Clarence Wharton, *Remember Goliad* (Glorieta, New Mexico: The Rio Grande Press, Inc., 1968), 47.

20. Pruett and Cole, Sr., *Goliad Massacre: A Tragedy of the Texas Revolution*, 109-113; and Webb. ed., *The Handbook of Texas*, 705; and Nell White, *Goliad in the Texas Revolution*, 48.

21. O'Connor, *The Presidio La Bahia del Espritu Santo de Zuniga 1721-1846*, 269; Nell White, *Goliad in the Texas Revolution*, 52; and Webb, ed., *The Handbook of Texas*, 705.

22. Benjamin Franklin Hughes in an account preserved (with spelling and punctuation corrections) among the Philip C. Tucker papers in the archives of the University of Texas, "Angel of Goliad," Texas State Archives.

23. Webb, ed., *The Handbook of Texas*, 705.

24. J.A. White, ed., *Dr. J.H. Barnard's Journal From December, 1835, to March 27th, 1836, Giving an Account of Fannin Massacre*, 27; and "Angel of Goliad," Texas State Archives.

25. Nell White, *Goliad in the Texas Revolution*, 48; and O'Connor, *The Presidio La Bahia del Espritu Santo de Zuniga 1721-1846*, 186-187, 215.

26. Hamilton, *Goliad Survivor: Isaac D. Hamilton*, 3, 9, 43-45, 50.

27. Pruett and Cole, Sr., *Goliad Massacre: A Tragedy of the Texas Revolution*, 35, 119; and O'Connor, *The Presidio La Bahia del Espritu Santo de Zuniga 1721-1846*, 119.

28. Hamilton, *Goliad Survivor: Isaac D. Hamilton*, 56-60.

29. J.A. White, ed., *Dr. J.H. Barnard's Journal From December, 1855, to March 27th, 1836, Giving an Account of Fannin Massacre*, 27.

30. "Angel of Goliad," Texas State Archives.

31. Ibid.; and Hamilton, *Goliad Survivor: Isaac D. Hamilton*, 63-64.

32. Ibid., 70-71.

33. Ibid., 66-71.

34. Webb, ed., *The Handbook of Texas*, 38.

35. Barnard used the name Sinora Alinez in his journal; Hughes and Brown used Alverez; Shackelford referred to her as Alevesco. Although she apparently spoke English, the Spanish sounds may have confused them. It would have been difficult to distinguish between Alvarez and Alavéz. "Angel of Goliad," Texas State Archives.

36. O'Connor, *The Presidio La Bahia del Espritu Santo de Zuniga 1721-1846*, 269; and Wharton, *Remember Goliad*, 47-48.

37. J.A. White, ed., *Dr. J.H. Barnard's Journal From December, 1835, to March 27th, 1836, Giving an Account of Fannin Massacre*, 26-27.

38. Henry Stuart Foote, *Texas and The Texans or, Advance of the Anglo-Americans to the Southwest; including A History of Leading Events in Mexico, from the Conquest by Fernando Cortes to the Termination of the Texan Revolution. In Two Volumes. Vol. II* (Philadelphia: Thomas, Cowperthwait & Co., 1841), 245.

39. Walraven, *The Magnificent Barbarians: Little Told Tales of the Texas Revolution*, 91, 96-98; and "Sequel of Angel of Goliad," Texas State Archives.

40. Walraven, *The Magnificent Barbarians: Little Told Tales of the Texas Revolution*, 97; and "Note by Father Joseph G. O'Donohoe," Texas State Archives.

Margarita Maza de Juárez
Grace and Courage

Years before the birth of Margarita Maza, twelve-year-old Benito Juárez appeared at the gate of her father's home in Oaxaca. Benito was barely three years old when he and his three sisters were orphaned by the death, in rapid succession, of both parents. The older children were placed with their paternal grandparents and a maternal aunt took the baby.

When their grandparents died a few years later, Benito went to live with his uncle in the nearby mountains. Bernardino Juárez, a poor farmer, scratched a meager living from the land and owned a small flock of sheep. The boy earned his keep as a shepherd and helped his uncle in the fields near their adobe hut. Bernardino taught his nephew the rudiments of reading and writing and stressed the importance of learning the Spanish language of which he had little, if any, knowledge.

Benito, a full-blooded Zapotec Indian, was keenly aware of his poverty. Considering the isolation of his rural community, he knew his chances of attending school were slim. Children raised in small villages rarely had even the most basic education. Parents with money for tuition and board sent their children to city schools. Other young people worked in private homes for a chance to learn to read and write.[1]

One day, a passing band of muleteers distracted the boy and stole one of his uncle's sheep. Benito, anticipating a beating, ran away from his uncle's home and traveled fourteen leagues to Oaxaca to search for his sister Josefa. He found her working as a cook for Don Antonio Maza and his wife, Petra Parada, who put him to work as a kitchen helper. A friendship, one that would last a lifetime, developed between the uneducated Indian boy who spoke only a few words of Spanish and the Mazas' son, José María.[2]

Benito was apprenticed to a Franciscan priest and bookbinder in exchange for his schooling. The boy studied diligently, suffering stoically the derisive comments of fellow students concerning his Indian heritage, his poverty, and ignorance. At the age of fifteen, he was enrolled in the seminary of Oaxaca to train for the priesthood. Although he excelled in his studies, Benito recognized theology was not for him and, before completing his studies at the seminary, decided to study law.[3]

A close relationship between the highly respected Maza family and Benito Juárez continued throughout his early years and into manhood. He was always welcome in their home and, on a visit in 1826, met the newest addition to the family: Margarita Eustaquia Maza Parada, born on the 28th of March. A baptismal certificate registered Margarita as a foundling adopted by Antonio Maza when her natural mother died in childbirth. However, on her marriage certificate, she was recorded as a "legitimate daughter" of the family.[4]

Margarita Maza de Juárez

From the Garcia Collection. Courtesy of the Nettie Lee Benson Latin American Collection. The General Libraries, The University of Texas at Austin.

Three factors influenced a girl during the first half of the nineteenth century: her home, her teachers, and the rigid customs of the times. Girls from affluent families, such as Margarita's, played freely in the nurseries, gardens, and patios of their spacious homes. However, by age twelve or thirteen, mothers began to admonish their daughters to behave as young women, although what this meant was not defined.[5]

The state of Oaxaca was greatly concerned with the education of children. There were *amigas* (elementary schools for girls) and secondary schools for those who could afford them. Typically, young women were taught to read, but not to write. This discouraged communication between sweethearts. They learned French, the language of culture, and to paint in watercolor. Even though they received instruction in music and singing, they did not perform outside the family confines. A proper upbringing also included training in domestic chores, but well-to-do women never practiced these because of numerous servants. This education best prepared young women of a certain social standing for a good marriage. Don Antonio, a *gachupín* of Italian heritage, was a product of different customs and believed these ideas to be outmoded. Nevertheless, Margarita was educated at home.[6]

Margarita was clearly intelligent. When she was thirteen, she helped her father keep his business books, answer his correspondence, and handle many routine tasks required of a good administrator. Her clear, readable script was an asset and was superior to that of Benito, the man she would later marry. Benito, who suffered from the results of a poor basic education, later spoke harshly of the country's inequitable instructional opportunities.[7]

By her seventeenth birthday, Margarita was a beautiful young woman with several suitors. Long dark hair framed her round face and her expression was warm and open. She was seriously courted by Carlos Corro, a wealthy Spanish merchant, and Antonio García, an army captain. Parents still arranged marriages for their daughters, but times were changing. Don Antonio allowed his daughter to choose her own Prince Charming, but her choice was neither a prince nor charming.[8]

Although the Mazas greatly admired Benito Juárez, there were many objections to Margarita marrying the dour-looking man. He was an Indian. He was thirty-seven years old, twenty years older than Margarita, and, whether or not they knew, had fathered two illegitimate children. Benito, a successful lawyer, rarely collected fees from his needy clients and could not offer Margarita the luxuries and security of her other suitors. In spite of these concerns, the Mazas recognized his many fine qualities. He was now a respected judge, and Margarita sincerely loved him.

The acceptance of Benito as a suitor for their daughter spoke highly for the Mazas and for society's lack of racial prejudice. There was nothing unusual about mestizo and Indian men marrying above their class, particularly if they aspired to a better life. This was a departure from the mores of colonial times and a sign of collapsing racial and caste barriers. The offspring of these unions were accepted as family members.[9]

"He is very homely, but very good," Margarita wrote to a friend about Benito. This aptly described the short, stocky man, with a scar across his wide face and a complexion darker than most Indians. He combed his heavy black hair stiffly across his forehead and his stern expression revealed nothing of his innate goodness.[10]

They were married August 1, 1843, in the church of San Felipi Neri in Oaxaca. Margarita wore satin and old lace; he dressed, as always, in a plain black suit. She called him Juárez; he called her his old lady.[11] Manuela, the first of their twelve children, was born in 1844, Felícitas followed in 1845, and Margarita, in 1848.

They were an extremely devoted couple, and though Benito remained unsmiling while engaged in official government business, at home he was a loving father and husband. Margarita and Benito lived in peace and harmony, but for Mexico it was a time of turmoil. Within the three years following their marriage, the presidency of the country changed many times during confrontations between the conservatives and the liberals, the church and the state.

In 1847 Benito was selected to complete a term as provisional governor of Oaxaca and dedicated himself to improving educational opportunities for the Indians. He was an able administrator and a just man. It was during this time that Benito tangled with Antonio López de Santa Anna. Although Santa Anna had been defeated by the Texans in their war for independence, he was committed to continuing the aggression. When the dictator fled from Mexico City to Oaxaca, Juárez refused to give him asylum. Twenty years earlier, when Benito was a young waiter serving at Santa Anna's table, the general had made disparaging remarks about Benito's Indian heritage.[12]

The next year, Benito was officially elected governor of the state. Hundreds of Indians came down from the mountains for his inauguration bringing gifts of fruit, corn, grain, and clucking chickens. That night, he and Margarita opened the doors of the governor's palace so the Indians might have a place to sleep. Each Indian left with a peso in the morning.[13]

When Don Antonio died in 1848, he bequeathed to Margarita a country house in the small village of Etla, not far from Oaxaca. At first, they used this as a weekend retreat, but as it seemed a better place to raise children than the dismal governor's mansion, they decided to make it their permanent home. There Margarita escaped the stress of political uncertainty in the capital and the daily news of Santa Anna's exploits. In spite of her distance from the unrest, Juárez had no wish to shield Margarita and he kept her informed about the realities of the times. She had no experience with politics or government, yet possessed great common sense and he valued her judgement. Over the years, she was a never-failing source of strength and serenity who always put his well-being before her own.[14]

During the next two years, Guadalupe and Soledad were born. When Guadalupe died at the age of two, Benito carried her small coffin to the civic cemetery which had been recently built outside the city walls to encourage sanitary burial. Hygiene was not always practiced or possible in traditional cemeteries belonging to the Church.[15] Margarita accepted her husband's decision to respect the law even though interment of government officials and influential people was still permitted within the churchyard. Again, the family put on the mourning costumes they had worn at the death of Don Antonio.

Amada was born in 1851 and was her father's favorite. This child, who would not sleep if he did not cradle her in his arms and sing her a lullaby, died at the age of three. Later another daughter, Francisca, died during infancy. In 1852, their first son, named Benito for his father and the only son to survive past childhood, was born.[16]

Juárez returned to his law practice after completing his term as governor. While riding along a desolate mountain road on May 27, 1853, he was apprehended and arrested by government soldiers. He was taken to the garrison at Jalapa in the mountains above Oaxaca, Santa Anna's ancestral estate, and held without charges for seventy-five days. Santa Anna never forgave Juárez for refusing him asylum in Oaxaca.

Then Benito was moved to San Juan Ulloa, near the coast of Veracruz, where he remained for twelve days before being placed aboard an outbound ship to Havana. Fellow passengers took up a collection to pay his fare and also covered the expense of a second passage to the United States. He arrived penniless in New Orleans and, for the next two years, rolled cigars in a tobacco factory with other Mexican liberals exiled by Santa Anna.[17]

Meanwhile, Margarita was forced to flee Etla because of harassment by her husband's enemies. She traveled to the mountains with the children who were carried in the arms of old Zapotec Indians. In a letter to Benito, she wrote about their visit to his uncle and the joy she and the children felt to see Laguna Encantada, the lake of his childhood.

After three months of living in the mountains, Margarita returned to Etla to make plans to support her family. She mortgaged her home and, with the money from the bank, opened a small store in her front parlor. She sold thread, bread, cigars, and sweets to sustain her family and sent Benito money to subsidize his meager income at the cigar factory. The people of Etla admired her determination and the shop became a success.[18]

In New Orleans, the exiles awaited political news from Mexico. After Santa Anna's final defeat, Benito's companions decided to combine their money to buy passage for his return to Mexico. They considered him to be the one most important to the new government. Upon arrival in Acapulco, Juárez was named minister of justice and public education in the new government forming under the leadership of Ignacio Comonfort. In 1857 Comonfort was elected president and Juárez was elected chief justice.[19]

Margarita and Benito reunited in Mexico City only to be separated again by his arrest by conservative troops in another government turnover. Comonfort, who had betrayed the liberals, then ordered his release, but Benito was forced to flee to Querétaro before alerting his family. This time, Margarita and the children sought refuge in Oaxaca. Comonfort resigned as president and Benito announced that, as chief justice and next in the line of succession, he was taking over as head of the country and setting up a new government capital in Veracruz.[20]

Margarita set out to join her husband. There were now eight children, the oldest, age fourteen, and the youngest, a baby. Twin daughters, María Josefa and María de Jesús, had been born in 1854 and a second son, José, called Pepito, was born in 1857. Margarita's brother, José María, accompanied them during this dangerous trip.

It took a month, traveling by night and hiding by day, to complete the 150-mile trip across the Sierra Madre. They walked and rode mules along rugged mountain paths where deep chasms threatened every step, and they lived on the food brought from home. Dense thickets echoed with sounds of unseen wild animals, and they feared attack by hungry beasts. Horsehair ropes were tied around the children as a safeguard on the perilous descent to the Rio Grande. At any moment, they could be surprised by bandits or enemy conservative soldiers. At last, guided only by the flickering light of oil lamps, they crossed the river in native boats. Not before they neared Veracruz did the liberal soldiers ride out to provide an escort.[21]

Benito was now a respected leader on his way to becoming a national hero. For the next three years, the country was divided by the conservative factions in Mexico City and the Juárez liberals in Veracruz. The United States was the only country to recognize the liberal government, which defeated the conservative army in 1860.

In 1861 Benito was elected president of Mexico, the first Indian to hold this office, and returned to Mexico City. The country was deeply in debt and England, France, and Spain had joined together to force payment. Juárez convinced the representatives from England and Spain of Mexico's inability to settle this debt, but France prepared to invade the country. French soldiers attacked the city of

Puebla in 1862 and, on May 5, crumbled under the might of the new Mexican nation, an event celebrated each year as *Cinco de Mayo.*[22]

A year later, France, with additional troops sent by Napoleon, defeated Juárez's army and Benito was forced to flee Mexico City again. During the summer of 1864, Benito and his cabinet moved to Monterrey where Margarita and the children lived in the ruins of a convent. Benito feared for his family's safety and decided to send them to the United States until the cessation of hostilities. There was another son now, Antonio, and their first grandchild. Margarita packed once more, taking only the necessities, and the family left the next day in an old black carriage held together by rope and wire. Their son-in-law, Pedro Santacilia, went along for protection, as soldiers could not be spared.[23]

Margarita was reluctant to leave Benito, but the fragile health of one of their sons and the absence of adequate medical attention in Mexico convinced her of the wisdom of her husband's decision. Margarita and ten children, the youngest an infant granddaughter, and her married daughter and son-in-law arrived in New York in November 1864. They settled modestly into a small house at 210 Thirteenth Street. Money was a problem for all Mexican refugees and diplomats in the United States, and they were no exception. After two months, a letter reached Benito with news of their safe arrival, lost luggage, and the boys' schooling.[24]

In January 1865, José died at the age of seven. In August, Antonio, their youngest son, died. In letters written to her husband during this period, she blamed herself for not giving her sons better care. She wrote of her constant tears and sorrow, which, she said, would cease only with her own death. The children may have died from cholera, which raged through the city of New York. Later, to escape the epidemic, the family moved to New

Rochelle. This new home, in a country setting, was an improvement and more like their place in Etla.

Although devastated from stress and grief, Margarita's first thoughts continued to be of Benito's well-being. Deeply anguished, she still worried about his health, whether he was eating properly, and the state of his clothing. She sent pictures of the family, but complained that she, turning forty and younger than he, now looked older.[25]

Matías Romero, the Mexican minister to the United States, had tried repeatedly to get Margarita to visit him in Washington. In March of 1866, believing she could help Romero's ailing mother, she agreed to travel to Washington with two of her daughters. Her daughter Margarita, now fairly fluent in English, acted as her interpreter. She spent a quiet week in the capital before news of her visit spread. Invitations arrived at the Romero house from officials eager to meet the wife of Mexico's president. At this time, the United States was interested in supporting Mexico's government in their war against the French. The Civil War in the United States had ended, but the country could do no more than offer diplomatic support.[26]

Margarita attended a grand reception at the White House, the first such affair held since the official mourning period following President Abraham Lincoln's assassination ended. A dinner in her honor was given at the home of William H. Seward, Secretary of State. Margarita's visit ended with a ball held in the home of General and Mrs. Ulysses S. Grant. President Andrew Johnson honored her with his presence. And even the French minister came, in spite of the fact that their countries were at war.[27]

For a short time, Margarita put aside her grief. In letters to Benito, she commented on the parties and the excessive expense when so many were needy. She also questioned the political knowledge of some government officials, as when William Seward remarked that he hoped to see his "two friends, Juárez and Santa Anna," together in Mexico. She told the Spanish minister, acting as her interpreter, to inform Mr. Seward that he "will see one or the other, not both."[28]

Mexican newspapers reported every detail of these events, contrasting them with the political conditions in their war-ravaged country. While liberal papers commented on her positive reception by the United States government, imperial papers took it as an opportunity to express their anger. When the American press described the rich gown and diamond jewelry she wore at the President's reception while her husband was in peril, she wrote to tell Juárez that this was not true. It distressed her that he might think she was living frivolously while he and the country suffered in poverty. She explained it was the dress he bought for her in Monterrey, which she saved for formal occasions, and her only jewels were earrings, a gift from him on her saint's day.[29]

Meanwhile, the situation in Mexico was grave. Juárez, torn by the war with France and Maximilian's determination to conquer Mexico, was deeply concerned with Margarita's health and her emotional stability. Fortunately, notes from the children with news of their successful school experiences and their progress with learning English brought him relief. On May 15, 1867, the French were finally defeated at Querétaro and Maximilian was captured.[30]

At last, Margarita was permitted to return to Mexico. President Johnson provided the American gunboat *Wilderness* for her trip. She arrived, dressed in mourning, with her only remaining son, Benito, and her five unmarried daughters. She brought the bodies of their two young sons for burial on Mexican soil. The citizens of Veracruz draped the city with flags and banners as crowds gathered to welcome her home. The golden coach of Maximilian was polished for her trip to the capital, but Margarita, overruling her children's delight, refused to ride in it. She preferred her husband's plain black coach. Along their route to Mexico City, countrymen cheered Margarita as the *primera dama de la Repúblic*. During one grand reception, she openly wept.[31]

Margarita's face was lined from grief and pain. The once robust woman grew frail and thin from an illness, which may have been cancer. Her family never revealed the exact nature of her final illness. She died on the afternoon of January 2, 1871, in their small house next to the church of San Cosme, at the age of forty-four. Juárez was inconsolable and allowed no one to touch her. He alone lifted her small body into the coffin. Then he needed to rest from the physical and emotional strain, as he had suffered a stroke nine months earlier and was not strong.

Juárez insisted on a secular funeral with only the family present. However, as the small procession moved to the cemetery, people appeared along the sides of the road in silent sympathy. His grief was private, but she was mourned by the world.[32]

When Margarita chose the somber Benito Juárez as her husband, she never envisioned life with a man destined to be a major force in her country's history. She withstood years of poverty, separation, and the deaths of five of her children, yet throughout these hardships maintained her quiet dignity. Their love was great, her courage profound.

NOTES ON CHAPTER EIGHT

1. W. Dirk Raat, ed., *Mexico: From Independence to Revolution, 1810-1910* (Lincoln, London: University of Nebraska Press, 1982), Benito Juárez, "Notes for my Children," 153-155.

2. Bob and Jan Young, *Liberators of Latin America* (New York: Lothrop, Lee & Shephard Co., 1970), 181; and James A. Magner, *Men of Mexico* (Freeport, New York: Books for Libraries Press, 1968), 351-352.

3. Magner, *Men of Mexico*, 353-354; and Ralph Roeder, *Juarez and His Mexico: A Biographical History, Vol. I* (New York: Greenwood Press, Publishers, 1968), 8-13, 46-47.

4. Carlos Velasco Pérez, *Margarita Maza de Juárez: Primera Dama de la Nación* (Mexico: Compañia Editorial del Papaloapan, S.A. de C.V., 1986), 14; and Charles Allen Smart, *Viva Juárez!* (Philadelphia: Lippincott, 1963), 69.

5. Angeles Mendieta Alatorre, *Margarita Maza de Juárez: Epistolario, antología, iconografía y efemérides* (Mexico: Comisión Nacional para la Conmemoración del Centenario del Fallecimiento de Don Benito Juárez, 1972), 23-24.

6. Ibid., 29-30; and Velasco Pérez, *Margarita Maza de Juárez: Primera Dama de la Nación*, 10-11; and Michael C. Meyer and William L. Sherman, *The Course of Mexican History: Third Edition* (New York, Oxford: Oxford University Press, 1987), 362.

7. Velasco Pérez, *Margarita Maza de Juárez: Primera Dama de la Nación*, 10-11; Raat, *Mexico From Independence to Revolution, 1810-1910*, Juárez, "Notes For My Children," 156.

8. Nina Brown Baker, *Juarez, Hero of Mexico* (New York: The Vanguard Press, 1942), 118-120; and Velasco Pérez, *Margarita Maza de Juárez: Primera Dama de la Nación*, 11-12.

9. Roeder, *Juarez and His Mexico: A Biographical History,* *Vol. I,* 66-67; Smart, *Viva Juárez!,* 68-69; T.R. Fehrenbach, *Fire and Blood: A History of Mexico* (New York: Macmillan Publishing Co., Inc., 1973), 406; and Jonathan Kandell, *La Capital: The Biography of Mexico City* (New York: Random House, 1988), 327.

10. Bob and Jan Young, *The Last Emperor: The Story of Mexico's Fight for Freedom* (New York: Julian Messner, 1969), 129-130.

11. Smart, *Viva Juárez!,* 69-70.

12. Kandell, *La Capital: The Biography of Mexico City,* 327.

13. Young, *Liberators of Latin America,* 185-186; Mendieta Alatorre, *Margarita Maza de Juárez: Epistolario, antología, iconografía y efemérides,* 37; and Smart, *Viva Juárez!,* 69-70.

14. Roeder, *Juarez and His Mexico: A Biographical History,* *Vol. II,* 549; and Baker, *Juarez, Hero of Mexico,* 133-134.

15. Jerome R. Adams, *Liberators and Patriots of Latin America: Biographies of 23 Leaders from Doña Marina (1505-1530) to Bishop Romero (1917-1980)* (Jefferson, North Carolina, and London: McFarland and Company, Inc., Publishers, 1991), 140.

16. Velasco Pérez, *Margarita Maza de Juárez: Primera Dama de la Nación,* 15.

17. Magner, *Men of Mexico,* 360; and Young, *Liberators of Latin America,* 186-187.

18. Ibid., 187; Baker, *Juárez, Hero of Mexico,* 168; Mendieta Alatorre, *Margarita Maza de Juárez: Epistolario, antología, iconografía y efemérides,* 38; and Velasco Pérez, *Margarita Maza de Juárez, Primera Dama de la Nación,* 21, 23.

19. Young, *Liberators of Latin America,* 188.

20. Ibid., 189-190.

21. Jasper Ridley, *Maximilian and Juárez* (New York: Ticknor & Fields, 1992), 33; Velasco Pérez, *Margarita*

Maza de Juárez: Primera Dama de la Nación, 29-32, 33; and Mendieta Alatorre, *Margarita Maza de Juárez: Epistolario, antología, iconografía y efemérides,* 40.

22. Young, *Liberators of Latin America,* 191-194.
23. Ibid., 194; and Baker, *Juarez, Hero of Mexico,* 256, 267.
24. Ridley, *Maximilian and Juárez,* 243; and Roeder, *Juarez and His Mexico, Vol. II,* 577-579.
25. Smart, *Viva Juárez!,* 361-362.
26. Young, *Liberators of Latin America,* 197.
27. Smart, *Viva Juárez!,* 363; and Ridley, *Maximilian and Juárez,* 243; and Roeder, *Juarez and His Mexico, Vol. II,* 633-634.
28. Smart, *Viva Juárez!,* 365.
29. Ibid, 364; Ridley, *Maximilian and Juárez,* 243; and Mendieta Alatorre, *Margarita Maza de Juárez: Epistolario, antología, iconografía y efemérides,* 47.
30. Young, *Liberators of Latin America,* 198-199.
31. Roeder, *Juarez and His Mexico,* 662; Mendieta Alatorre, *Margarita Maza de Juárez: Epistolario, antología, iconografía y efemérides,* 48-49; and Baker, *Juarez, Hero of Mexico,* 289, 292, 295.
32. Roeder, *Juarez and His Mexico,* 715-716; and Smart, *Viva Juárez!,* 405-406.

GLOSSARY

cacique/cacica - Indian chief, used by the Spaniards to refer to one of power

china - servant girl of Indian or mestizo blood

conquistador - conqueror

corregidor/corregidora - local magistrate

creole - offspring born in Mexico to Spanish parents

escribiano - notary public or clerk

gachupín - literally "wearer of spurs," used derisively to refer to the Spanish

grito - cry or shout

guadalupes - insurgents who adopted the image of the Virgin of Guadalupe as their banner

haciendado - owner of an estate

huipil - woman's long, sleeveless blouse, still worn in parts of Mexico

insurgentes - insurgent, rebel

mestizo - offspring of European and Indian heritage

metate - curved or flat stone used from grinding maize for tortillas or cocoa for chocolate

Nauhatl - language, also known as Aztec or Mexican

peninsulares - those born in Spain

poblano - one belonging to a village

pulque - an intoxicant, fermented milk of the maguez cactus

quetzal - a large, brilliantly colored Central American bird worshipped by the Aztecs and Mayas as the god Quetzalcoatl

rebozo - woman's shawl

recogimientos - house where women are confined or live in retirement

BIBLIOGRAPHY

Adams, Jerome R. *Liberators and Patriots of Latin America: Biographies of 23 Leaders from Doña Marina (1505-1530) to Bishop Romero (1917-1980)*. Jefferson, North Carolina, and London: McFarland & Company, Inc., Publishers, 1991.

Agraz García de Alba, Gabriel. *Los Corregidores Don Miguel Domínguez y Doña María Josefa Ortiz y el inicio de la independencia. Tomo I*. Mexico, D.F.: Edición del Autor, 1992.

Baker, Nina Brown. *Juarez, Hero of Mexico*. New York: The Vanguard Press, 1942.

Bancroft, Hubert Howe. *History of Mexico, Volume XII, Vol. IV, 1804-1824*. San Francisco: The History Company, Publishers, 1886.

Bancroft, Hubert Howe. *History of the North American States and Texas*, Volume II. San Francisco: The History Company, Publishers, 1899.

Barr, Alwyn. *Texans in Revolt: The Battle for San Antonio, 1835*. Austin: University of Texas Press, 1990.

Bazant, Jan. *A Concise History of Mexico from Hidalgo to Cárdenas, 1805-1940*. Cambridge, London, New York, Melbourne: Cambridge University Press, 1977.

Berdan, Frances F. *Indians of North America: The Aztecs*. New York, Philadelphia: Chelsea House Publishers, 1989.

Berler, Beatrice. *The Conquest of Mexico: A Modern Rendering of William H. Prescott's History*. San Antonio: Corona Publishing Company, 1988.

Blacker, Irwin R. *Cortés and the Aztec Conquest*. New York: American Heritage Publishing Co., Inc., 1965.

Bleeker, Sonia. *The Aztec Indians of Mexico.* New York: William Morrow & Co., 1963.

Borton de Trevino, Elizabeth. *Here Is Mexico.* New York: Farrar, Straus & Giroux, 1970.

Bray, Warwick. *Everyday Life of the Aztecs.* London: B.T. Batsford Ltd., and New York: G.P. Putnam's Sons, 1968.

Chinchilla Pawling, Perla, colaboración. *Leona Vicario.* Serie de Cuadernos Conmemorativos, Comisión Nacional para las Celebraciónes del 175 Aniversario de la Independencia Nacional y 75 Aniversario de la Revolución Mexicana. Mexico: Instituto Nacional de Estudios Históricos de la Revolución Mexicana, Col. Juárez, C.P., 1985.

Coe, Michael D. *Ancient Peoples and Places: Mexico.* New York: Frederick A. Praeger, Publisher, 1962.

Collis, Maurice. *Cortés and Montezuma.* London: Faber and Faber, mcmliv.

Cotera, Martha. *Profile on the Mexican American Woman.* Austin, Texas: National Educational Laboratory Publishers, Inc., 1976.

Crow, John A. *The Epic of Latin America, Revised Edition.* Garden City, New York: Doubleday & Company, Inc., 1971.

Cypess, Sandra Messinger. *La Malinche in Mexican Literature: From History to Myth.* Austin: University of Texas Press, 1991.

De Fuentes, Patricia, ed. and tr. *The Conquistadors.* New York: The Orion Press, Inc., 1963.

Díaz del Castillo, Bernal. *The Discovery and Conquest of Mexico, 1517-1521.* London: George Routledge & Sons, Ltd., 1928.

Díaz del Castillo, Captain Bernal. *The True History of the Conquest of Mexico.* Translated from original Spanish by Maurice Keatinge. New York: Robert M. McBride & Company, 1927.

Diccionario Porrúa, Historia, Geografía y Biographías de Mexico, Vol. II. Mexico: Editorial Porrua, S.A., 1981.

Echánove-Trujillo, C.A. *Leona Vicario: La Mujer Fuerte de la Independencia.* Mexico: Ediciones, Xochitl, 1945.

Elfer, Maurice. *Madam Candelaria: Unsung Heroine of the Alamo.* Houston, Texas: The Rein Company, Publishers, 1933.

Enciclopedia de México, Tomo II, Tomo VIII, Tomo X. Ciudad de México, S.A.: Instituto de la Enciclopedia de México, 1974.

Fehrenbach, T.R. *Fire and Blood: A History of Mexico.* New York: Macmillan Publishing Co., Inc., 1973.

Fernández de Lizardi, J.J. *Heroinas mexicanas.* Mexico: Biblioteca de Historiadores Mexicanos, 1955.

Fisher, Howard T. and Marion Hall Fisher, eds. and anns. *Life in Mexico: The Letters of Fanny Calderón de la Barca with New Material from the Author's Private Journals.* Garden City, New York: Doubleday & Company, Inc., 1966.

Foote, Henry Stuart. *Texas and The Texans or, Advance of the Anglo-Americans to the Southwest; including A History of Leading Events in Mexico, from the Conquest by Fernando Cortes to the Termination of the Texan Revolution. In Two Volumes. Vol. II.* Philadelphia: Thomas, Cowperthwait & Co., 1841.

Friedrichs, Irene Hohmann. *History of Goliad.* Victoria, Texas: Regal Printers, 1961.

García, Genaro. *Leona Vicario: heroina insurgente.* Mexico: Editorial Innovacion, S.A., 1910.

García Rivas, Heriberto. *Biografias de Mexicanos Ilustres.* Mexico: Grupo Editorial Diana, S.A., Universaro, 1962.

González Peña, Carlos. Gusta Barfield Nance and Florene Johnson Dunstan, trs. *History of Mexican Literature: Third Edition.* Dallas: Southern Methodist Press, 1968.

Goodspeed, Bernice I. *Mexican Tales.* Mexico, D.F.: American Book & Printing Co., S.A., 1946.

Green, Stanley C. *The Mexican Republic: The First Decade 1823-1832*. Pittsburgh, PA: University of Pittsburgh Press, 1987.

Gruening, Ernest. *Mexico and Its Heritage*. New York: Appleton-Century-Crofts, Inc., 1928.

Hamill, Jr., Hugh M. *The Hidalgo Revolt: Prelude to Mexican Independence*. Gainesville: University of Florida Press, 1966.

Hamilton, Lester. *Goliad Survivor: Isaac D. Hamilton*. San Antonio, Texas: The Naylor Company, 1971.

Henderson, James D. and Linda Roddy Henderson. *Ten Notable Women of Latin America*. Chicago: Nelson-Hall, 1942.

House, Boyce. *San Antonio: City of Flaming Adventure*. San Antonio, Texas: The Naylor Company, 1968.

Hughes, Jill. *Aztecs*. New York: Gloucester Press, 1986.

Idell, Albert, tr. and ed. *The Bernal Díaz Chronicles: The True Story of the Conquest of Mexico*. Garden City, New York: Doubleday & Company, 1957.

Johnson, William Weber. *Cortés*. Boston, Toronto: Little, Brown and Company, 1975.

Kandell, Jonathan. *La Capital: The Biography of Mexico City*. New York: Random House, 1988.

Kubiak, Daniel James. *Ten Tall Texans*. San Antonio, Texas: The Naylor Company, 1970.

Larralde, Elsa. *The Land and People of Mexico*. Philadelphia and New York: J.B. Lippincott Company, 1964.

Lechuga, Ruth D. *El Traje Indígena de Mexico*. Mexico, D.F.: Panorama Editorial, S.A., 1986.

Leon-Portilla, Miguel. *Broken Spears: The Aztec Account of the Conquest of Mexico*. Boston: Beacon Press, 1962.

López de Gómara, Francisco. *Córtes, The Life of the Conqueror by His Secretary*. Translated and Edited by Lesley Byrd Simpson from the "Istoria de la Conquista de Mexico," Zaragoza, 1552. Berkeley: University of California Press, 1964.

Lord, Walter. *A Time to Stand*. New York: Harper & Row, Publishers, 1961.

MacLachlan, Colin M. and Jaime E. Rodriguez O. *The Forging of the Cosmic Race: A Reinterpretation of Colonial Mexico*. Berkeley, Los Angeles, London: University of California Press, 1980.

McClintock, Marshall, *Prescott's The Conquest of Mexico, Designed for Modern Reading*. New York: Jullian Messner, 1948.

McNeer, May and Lynd Ward. *The Mexican Story*. New York: Ariel Books, 1953.

Magner, James A. *Men of Mexico*. Freeport, New York: Books for Libraries Press, 1968.

Marrin, Albert. *Aztecs and Spaniards: Cortes and the Conquest of Mexico*. New York: Atheneum, 1986.

Maza, Francisco de la. *Catarina de San Juan: princesa de la India y visionaria de Puebla*. Elisa Vargaslugo, prologo. Cien de Mexico. Mexico, D.F.: Consejo Nacional para la Cultura y las Artes, Dirección General de Comunicaciones, 1990.

Mendieta Alatorre, Angeles. *Margarita Maza de Juárez: Epistolario, antología, iconografía y efemérides*. Mexico: Comisión Nacional para la Conmemoración del Centenario del Fallecimiento de Don Benito Juárez, 1972.

Merrim, Stephanie, ed. *Feminist Perspectives on Sor Juana Inés de la Cruz*. Detroit: Wayne State University, 1991. Asunción Lavrin. "Unlike Sor Juana? The Model Nun in the Religious Literature of Colonial Mexico." Dorothy Schons. "Some Obscure Points in the Life of Sor Juana Inés de la Cruz."

Meyer, Michael C. and William L. Sherman. *The Course of Mexican History: Third Edition*. New York, Oxford: Oxford University Press, 1987.

Miquel i Vergés, José María. *Diccionario de insurgentes*. Mexico: Editorial Porrúa, 1969.

Miller, Beth, ed. *Women in Hispanic Literature: Icons and Fallen Idols.* Berkeley: University of California Press, 1983.

Moreland, W.H. and Atul Chandra Chatterjee. *A Short History of India: Fourth Edition.* New York: David McKay Company, Inc., 1957.

Nava, Julian. *Mexican Americans Past, Present, and Future.* New York: American Book Company, Litton Educational Publishing, Inc., 1969.

Nicholson, Irene. *The Liberators: A Study of Independence Movements in Spanish America.* New York, Washington: Frederick A. Praeger, Publishers, 1969.

Noll, Arthur Howard and A. Phillip McMahon. *The Life and Times of Miguel Hidalgo y Costilla.* Chicago: A.C. McClurg & Co., 1910.

O'Connor, Kathryn Stoner. *The Presidio La Bahia del Espritu Santo de Zuniga 1721 to 1846.* Austin, Texas: Von Boeckmann-Jones Co., 1966.

Paz, Octavio. Margaret Sayre Peden, tr. *Sor Juana Or, The Traps of Faith.* Cambridge, Massachusetts: The Belknap Press of Harvard University Press, 1988.

Potter, R.M. *The Fall of the Alamo: A Reminiscence of the Revolution of Texas.* San Antonio: Herald Steam Press, 1860. Reprinted by Fuller Printing Company: Bryan, Texas, 1979.

Potter, Reuben M. *The Fall of The Alamo.* With an Introduction and Notes by Charles Grosvenor. Hillsdale, New Jersey: The Otterden Press, 1977.

Prescott, William H. *History of the Conquest of Mexico, Vol. III.* New York: Harper and Brothers, 1843.

Pruett, Jakie L. and Everett B. Cole, Sr. *Goliad Massacre: A Tragedy of the Texas Revolution.* Austin, Texas: Eakin Press, 1985.

Raat, W. Dirk, ed. *Mexico: From Independence to Revolution, 1810-1910.* Lincoln and London: University of Nebraska Press, 1982.

Ragsdale, Crystal Sasse. *The Women and Children of the Alamo.* Austin, Texas: State House Press, 1994.

Rawlinson, H.G. *India: A Short Cultural History.* New York: Frederick A. Praeger, 1952.

Ridley, Jasper. *Maximilian and Juárez.* New York: Ticknor & Fields, 1992.

Robinson, Henry Morton. *Stout Cortez: A Biography of the Spanish Conquest.* New York: The Century Co., 1931.

Rodman, Selden. *A Short History of Mexico.* New York: Stein and Day, 1982.

Roeder, Ralph. *Juarez and His Mexico: A Biographical History, Volume I and Volume II.* New York: The Viking Press, Inc., 1947, reprinted New York: Greenwood Press, Publishers, 1968.

Rosenblum, Morris. *Heroes of Mexico.* New York: Fleet Press Corporation, 1969.

Ross, Sir E. Denison and Eileen Power, eds. F. Bayard Morris, tr. *Hernando Cortés: Five Letters, 1519-1526.* London: George Routledge & Sons, Ltd., 1928.

Salas, Elizabeth. *Soldaderas in the Mexican Military: Myth and History.* Austin: University of Texas Press, 1990.

Santos, Richard G. *Santa Anna's Campaign Against Texas, 1835-1836, Featuring the Field Commands Issued to Major General Vicente Filisola.* Salisbury, North Carolina: Texian Press, 1968.

Schoelwer, Susan Prendergast, with Tom W. Glaser. *Alamo Images: Changing Perceptions of a Texas Experience.* Dallas, Texas: The DeGolyer Library and Southern Methodist University Press, 1985.

Schwarz, Ted. *Forgotten Battlefield of the First Texas Revolution: The Battle of Medina, August 18, 1813.* Austin, Texas: Eakin Press, 1985.

Smart, Charles Allen. *Viva Júarez!* Philadelphia: Lippincott, 1963.

Sturmberg, Robert. *History of San Antonio and of the Early Days in Texas*. San Antonio, Texas: St. Joseph's Society Press of the Standard Printing Co., 1920.

Tamayo, Jorge L. *Antologia de Benito Júarez*. Mexico: Universidad Nacional Autonoma de Mexico, 1972.

Tavard, George H. *Juana Inés de la Cruz and the Theology of Beauty: The First Mexican Theology*. Notre Dame, London: University of Notre Dame Press, 1991.

The Columbia Encyclopedia, Second Edition. Morningside Heights, New York: Columbia University Press, 1950.

The World Book Encyclopedia, Volume 13. Chicago, London, Paris, Sydney, Tokyo, Toronto: World Book-Childcraft International, Inc., 1980.

The Texas Almanac for 1859 with Statistics, Historical & Biographical Sketches &C. Relating to Texas. Galveston: Richardson & Co.

Thomas, Hugh. *Conquest: Montezuma, Cortés, and the Fall of Old Mexico*. New York, London, Toronto, Sydney, Tokyo, Singapore: Simon & Schuster, 1993.

Tinkle, Lon. *13 Days to Glory: The Siege of the Alamo*. New York: McGraw-Hill Book Company, Inc., 1958.

Toor, Frances. *A Treasury of Mexican Folkways*. New York: Crown Publishers, 1947.

Torner, Florentino M. *Creadores De La Imagen Historica De Mexico*. Mexico, D.F.: Compania General de Ediciones, S.A., 1971.

Torres-Ríoseco, Arturo. *The Epic of Latin American Literature*. Berkeley, Los Angeles, and London: University of California Press, 1970.

Trueblood, Alan S., tr. *A Sor Juana Anthology*. Cambridge, Massachusetts and London, England: Harvard University Press, 1988.

Velasco Pérez, Carlos. *Margarita Maza de Juárez: Primera Dama de la Nación*. Mexico: Compañia Editorial del Papaloapan, S.A. de C.V., 1986.

Vigness, David M. *The Revolutionary Decades.* Austin, Texas: Steck-Vaughn Company, 1965.

Walraven, Bill and Marjorie K. *The Magnificent Barbarians: Little Told Tales of the Texas Revolution.* Austin, Texas: Eakin Press, 1993.

Webb, Walter Prescott, ed. *The Handbook of Texas.* Austin: The Texas State Historical Association, 1952.

Wharton, Clarence. *Remember Goliad.* Glorieta, New Mexico: The Rio Grande Press, Inc., 1968.

White, J.A., ed. *Dr. J.H. Barnard's Journal, from December, 1835, to March 27th, 1836, Giving an Account of Fannin Massacre.* Goliad, Texas: *Goliad Advance,* 1912. Reproduced by J.A. White Family, 1988.

White, Jon Manchip. *Cortes and the Downfall of the Aztec Empire: A Study in a Conflict of Cultures.* New York: St. Martin's Press, 1971.

White, Nell. *Goliad in the Texas Revolution,* A Thesis Presented to the Faculty of the Graduate School University of Houston, May, 1941. Eakin Publications, Inc., Austin, Texas, 1988.

Young, Bob and Jan. *The Last Emperor: The Story of Mexico's Fight for Freedom.* New York: Julian Messner, 1969.

Young, Bob and Jan. *Liberators of Latin America.* New York: Lothrop, Lee & Shepard Co., 1970.

Zabre, Alfonso Teja. *Guide to the History of Mexico: A Modern Interpretation.* Austin, New York: The Pemberton Press, Jenkins Publishing Company, 1969.

Zárate, Verónica, colaboración. *Josefa Ortiz de Domínguez: La Corregidora.* Serie de Cuadernos Conmemorativos, Comisión Nacional para las Celebraciones del 175 Aniversario de la Independencia Nacional y 75 Aniversario de la Revolución Mexicana. Mexico: Instituto Nacional de Estudios Históricos de la Revolución Mexicana, Col. Juárez, C.P., 1985.

PRINTED MATERIAL

Elfer, Maurice. "Madame Candelaria, Unsung Heroine of the Alamo Nursed Bowie to the End." *The Dallas Morning News*, March 9, 1930.

Madame Candelaria Files. Daughters of the Republic of Texas Library at the Alamo.

San Antonio *Daily Express*, February 11, 1899. "The Last Voice Hushed: Death of Madam Candelaria Yesterday."

Texas State Archives. "Angel of Goliad," "Sequel of Angel of Goliad," and "Note by Father Joseph G. O'Donohoe."

"The story of the Alamo: Thirteen fateful days in 1836," The Daughters of the Republic of Texas.

INDEX

Other Books From Republic of Texas Press

*100 Days in Texas: The Alamo
Letters*
by Wallace O. Chariton

*At Least 1836 Things You
Ought to Know About Texas
but Probably Don't*
by Doris L. Miller

*Classic Clint: The Laughs and
Times of Clint Murchison, Jr.*
by Dick Hitt

*Country Savvy: Survival Tips
for Farmers, Ranchers, and
Cowboys*
by Reed Blackmon

Critter Chronicles
by Jim Dunlap

Dallas Uncovered
by Larenda Lyles Roberts

*Defense of a Legend: Crockett
and the de la Peña Diary*
by Bill Groneman

*Dirty Dining: A Cookbook, and
More, for Lovers*
by Ginnie Siena Bivona

*Don't Throw Feathers at
Chickens: A Collection of Texas
Political Humor*
by Charles Herring, Jr. and
Walter Richter

*Eight Bright Candles:
Courageous Women of Mexico*
by Doris E. Perlin

*Exotic Pets: A Veterinary Guide
for Owners*
by Shawn Messonnier, D.V.M.

Exploring the Alamo Legends
by Wallace O. Chariton

*From an Outhouse to the White
House*
by Wallace O. Chariton

The Funny Side of Texas
by Ellis Posey and John
Johnson

Ghosts Along the Texas Coast
by Docia Schultz Williams

*The Great Texas Airship
Mystery*
by Wallace O. Chariton

*Great Texas Golf: A Complete
Directory to All Texas Golf
Courses*
by Pat Seelig

*How the Cimarron River Got
Its Name and Other Stories
About Coffee*
by Ernestine Sewell Linck

*I Never Wanted to Set the
World on Fire, but Now That
I'm 50 Maybe It's a Good Idea*
by Bob Basso, Ph.D.

Just Passing Through
by Beth Beggs

Kingmakers
by John R. Knaggs

Call for names of the bookstores in your area
(214) 423-0090

Other Books From Republic of Texas Press

The Last Great Days of Radio
by Lynn Woolley

Los Angeles Uncovered
by Frank Thompson

Mastering Magic Cards
by George H. Baxter and Larry
W. Smith, Ph.D.

*Noble Brutes: Camels on the
American Frontier*
by Eva Jolene Boyd

Only: The Last Dinosaur
by Jim Dunlap

*Outlaws in Petticoats and
Other Notorious Texas Women*
by Ann Ruff and Gail Drago

Rainy Days in Texas Funbook
by Wallace O. Chariton

San Antonio Uncovered
by Mark Louis Rybczyk

Slitherin' 'Round Texas
by Jim Dunlap

*Spirits of San Antonio and
South Texas*
by Docia Schultz Williams and
Reneta Byrne

Texas Highway Humor
by Wallace O. Chariton

*Texas Politics in My Rearview
Mirror*
by Waggoner Carr and Byron
Varner

*Texas Tales Your Teacher
Never Told You*
by Charles F. Eckhardt

Texas Wit and Wisdom
by Wallace O. Chariton

That Cat Won't Flush
by Wallace O. Chariton

*That Old Overland
Stagecoaching*
by Eva Jolene Boyd

They Don't Have to Die
by Jim Dunlap

This Dog'll Hunt
by Wallace O. Chariton

To the Tyrants Never Yield
by Kevin R. Young

*Tragedy at Taos: The Revolt of
1847*
by Jim Crutchfield

A Trail Rider's Guide to Texas
by Mary Elizabeth Sue
Goldman

Twin Cities Uncovered
by The Arthurs

Unsolved Texas Mysteries
by Wallace O. Chariton

Western Horse Tales
Edited by Don Worcester

Wild Camp Tales
by Mike Blakely

Your Puppy's First Year
by Shawn Messonnier, D.V.M.

Call for names of the bookstores in your area
(214) 423-0090